COUNTERFEIT
I.D.
MADE EASY

Jack Luger is author of these other fine books available from Loompanics Unlimited:

- *Code Making and Code Breaking*
- *Improvised Weapons in American Prisons*
- *How to Use Mail Drops for Privacy and Profit*
- *The Big Book of Secret Hiding Places*

COUNTERFEIT I.D. MADE EASY

Jack Luger

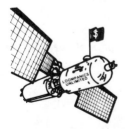

Loompanics Unlimited
Port Townsend, Washington

COUNTERFEIT I.D. MADE EASY

© 1990 by Jack Luger
Printed in USA

Published by:
Loompanics Unlimited
PO Box 1197
Port Townsend, WA 98368

Illustrations by Shellay Herman

ISBN 0-915179-90-3
Library of Congress
   Catalog Card Number 90-060515

Contents

1

Introduction:

What This Book Will Do for You

This book will do two things for you: 1) Show you how people make and use fake I.D. and 2) Help to keep you from becoming their victim.

Let's start by stating one basic fact: It's not illegal to change names, as long as it's not for a fraudulent purpose. Divorced persons sometimes do this to elude former spouses who still chase after them in hope of reconciliation.

"Getting in" to various places sometimes requires counterfeit I.D. Some people want to get into a bar if they're under-age, or cash a check. Counterfeit I.D. is also used by people to rent Post Office boxes or mail drop boxes. It can also be used to buy a firearm.

Sometimes, I.D. can be counterfeited without infringing any law, as we'll see. Counterfeiting is not necessarily illegal.

What about the consequences of making such knowledge public? Isn't it a serious error to release techniques that can be used by criminals for fraudulent purposes? The answers, like the questions, are simple:

First, criminals already know how to forge documents. Novices get personalized instruction at our publicly-funded schools for crime —

our prisons. These institutions, originally set up to punish and to "rehabilitate" criminals, provide post-graduate courses in criminal technology.

Secondly, forged documents don't comprise much of the crime. For example, fraud and "insider" abuse have been the causes of much larger dollar losses than fake bank cards.[1] The small-time crook who steals with a fake bank card makes off with very little compared to the bank executive who turns dishonest and, by manipulating a system whose weaknesses he knows intimately, gets away with very large sums.

Making and using counterfeit I.D. is both a lot simpler and a lot more dangerous than many people realize. This is because modern methods of photo-reproduction make counterfeiting I.D. very quick and easy. It's dangerous because using fake I.D. can get you into a lot of trouble.

The authorities have devised some very sophisticated means of verifying the authenticity of I.D. Those who would use forged I.D. can get into very serious trouble if they try to go too far.

We'll discuss what goes into I.D., the limitations of forgery, and the measures taken by the authorities to defeat forgeries. You'll find out exactly how criminals make and use counterfeit I.D., and how they avoid detection and prosecution.

Sources

1. *Washington Post,* article by Kathleen Day, November 21, 1987.

2

Serving Different Purposes

There are many reasons people use a counterfeit identity, and many are perfectly legal. A simple example is that of a person who frequents the "singles bar scene." These are for quick and temporary relationships, not long-term affairs, but not everyone understands this. Using a false name is one way of eluding persistent romancers who may call at all hours.

Employment

A more serious need is earning a living. An illegal alien, under the new immigration laws, will find this more difficult than ever. Fake I.D. is often used to gain entrance into the United States and to find employment once here.

Even for citizens, finding employment is not an easy task. This is an area where quick-and-dirty forgeries are commonplace. They may be used to cover up a gap in employment history. A person fired from a job may not want to list that employer. A person who spent 90 days in jail on a drunk driving charge may want to cover that gap. A faked letter of recommendation might fill the gap. If it's from an out-of-town firm, this further reduces the chances that a confirming telephone call will be made.

Test Cheating

One way students have beaten the Scholastic Aptitude Test, or S.A.T., is by having a "ringer" take the test for them. Test proctors don't know each student personally, and often ask to see I.D. The cheaply produced laminated cards issued by most high schools are not tamper-proof. It's easy for a student to slit the plastic laminate, lay the "ringer's" photo on top of his, then re-seal the card.

Sex

Adultery is illegal in some states. In others, the law is silent. It doesn't have to be a felony for an adulterous experience to cause trouble. Some hard-boiled prostitutes frequent conventions to find people who seek extra-marital sex. It only takes a couple of compromising photographs to conduct a blackmail racket. A conventioneer who wants to protect himself would be wise to leave his wallet in his hotel room and use a false name when making a "pickup."

Some people carry on lengthy extra-marital affairs. These might involve frequent correspondence which is inconvenient to get at home. This is where the mail drop becomes useful. It further shrouds the identity when it's rented under a false name.

There are some sexual tastes which can ruin the reputation if generally known. This is why some people rent mail drops under false names — to receive books and magazines that arrive in "plain brown wrappers." Likewise, if they get into dangerous games such as pedophilia, and join one of the pedophilia clubs in this country, they often use fake names.

Most sex clubs publish membership directories because their purpose is to put members "in touch" with one another. If the nature of the club suggests illegal activity, or if the member lives in a locale where knowledge of his membership could cause him serious trouble, he'd be wise to use a false name.

Passing for Over-21

A boy who looks like he's 21, but is really only 18, might want to get into a bar or to buy liquor at a supermarket. Because the state laws on sale of alcohol are so strict, bar owners and store clerks typically ask for I.D. of anyone who looks under 30. They're not taking any chances. Passing for 21 is where the forged or borrowed drivers license is commonly used and seldom questioned.

The same goes for adult book stores. Their owners don't want to face a mob of angry parents for allowing children to view their material, so they usually require I.D. from anyone who seems under-age.

Post Office Box Rentals

You have to show some I.D. to rent a post office box. This also applies to those seeking to rent a private mail box, known as a "mail drop." Postal regulations require it, and there's no legal way around it. A few mail drop operators don't ask for I.D., but that's rare.

Banking

I.D. is now required to open a bank account or to rent a safe deposit box in a bank. Those who are trying to stash money or materials they don't want the government to find often use private vaults. Operators of these private vaults are not regulated the way banks are, and are likely to be hostile to government surveillance and interference. Typically, they don't demand I.D.

Buying Weapons

The Federal Gun Control Act of 1968 mandates that all weapons sold must be registered by the dealer, who fills out a "Form 4473" on the purchaser. Unless the buyer is known personally to the dealer, there must be I.D. shown for verification of identity. This is usually a drivers license, and the type and serial number of the I.D. must be recorded on the form. Because many firearms dealers are not in agreement with the intent of the gun control law, they tend to be pretty lenient in accepting I.D.

Passport

Fictitious I.D. is commonly used to obtain a passport. Because U.S. citizens are often targets for terrorists and hijackers, many Americans want a Canadian passport.[1] Canada keeps a low profile, and doesn't send troops around the world to intervene in the affairs of other countries. Also, Americans can easily pass for Canadians, especially to citizens of other countries.

Forgery in Prison

Even prison inmates forge documents. Many state prisons have print shops, and some state prison shops print official documents to save the state the cost of having them commercially printed. In one prison, inmates diverted some of the guards' meal ticket books and sold them "under the counter" to guards for currency, which was contraband.[2]

Prisoners who work in the print shop as "rehabilitation" often take the opportunity to create fake documents for use in the outside world. Some forge birth certificates, baptismal certificates, and other official paperwork. In one case, inmates counterfeited prison release papers, and managed to get them into the prison paperwork pipeline. This resulted in the premature release of several prisoners.

There's hardly any limit to the uses, public or private, forged documents have been put to. Not all of the uses are harmless, and most are illegal.

Sources

1. *Vanish! Disappearing through I.D. Acquisition,* Johnny Yount, Boulder, CO, Paladin Press, 1986, pp. 78-79.

2. *The Inmate Economy,* David B. Kalinich, Lexington, MA, Lexington Books, 1980, p. 20.

3

The Wide Spectrum of Fake I.D.

I'll start by defining "fake I.D." This is any paperwork that does not legitimately belong to the holder, or which misrepresents the holder's identity or accomplishments. Now you'll better understand exactly where forged I.D. fits in, and how it is used.

Stolen I.D.

Stolen I.D. is very limited. In Twentieth-Century America, it's used mainly by criminals. Plastic bank cards are of limited value to the criminal, because to get money out of an automatic teller machine, it's necessary to punch in a personal identification code. Cashing checks often requires two pieces of I.D., one of which must have a photograph. It's stretching coincidence too far for a criminal to expect to steal I.D. from a look-alike.

Paper-Tripping

This is the elaborate "infant I.D." method, in which the identity-changer finds the name and birth-place of someone approximately his own age, but who died young, and obtains his birth certificate as a beginning to a new identity. Although this method is very old, it still works today because most government records departments don't void out birth certificates when an individual dies. The whole point of "paper-tripping" is to obtain a fake identity with genuine documents. It requires work to fully document this identity, so this method is too elaborate for most people seeking fake I.D.

Purchased Documents

Money can buy almost anything, including fake documents of varying quality. Classified ads in some of the tabloids offer diplomas for sale. Through word of mouth, it is relatively easy to come across a forger who will make the documents you need for the right price. One could also obtain forged passports through a connection with "organized crime."

All of these possibilities create two problems for the purchaser. One is that his secret is no longer his alone. Someone else knows, and this can be dangerous for him. The other problem is that some of these fake document operations are government "stings."

Any sort of purchased document has an additional problem. It can not be "backstopped," and this can get the user into very serious trouble. We'll cover backstopping in a later chapter.

Purchased documents rarely fill the needs of those who want fake I.D. That's why many identity-seekers prefer the "do-it-yourself" methods.

Counterfeit

This is the do-it-yourself method that works amazingly well for those with moderate dexterity and skill. That's what this book is all about.

4

Backstopping:

Making the Image Real

A piece of I.D., plastic or paper, is only that, and doesn't in itself prove very much. It can pass only a quick inspection if it's not real. Providing additional dimensions to an assumed identity that can stand up to an investigation is called "backstopping." We'll get into this topic to show you what happens when people using fake I.D. try to reach too far. You'll learn how they create additional support for their fake identity. We'll also see where backstopping can work without the actual I.D. papers.

Let's start with a case-by-case examination of why and how backstopping is necessary in certain instances. We'll start with fairly simple cases, and work our way up to "Mission Impossible."

"John" is stopped for a traffic offense by a police officer, and presents a fake drivers license. It's normal police procedure today to radio the information in for a computerized check by the motor vehicle and drivers license bureaus. If the license John presents is totally forged, the officer will soon get a message back stating that there is no record of such a license, and John will have to answer some severe questions. If the license is real, belonging to someone who resembles John but who lost it, the radio check may not expose him.

An exception can be if the person has reported the license lost or stolen.

John applies for a library card, using his fake I.D. He shows the librarian his drivers license and his birth certificate in the name of "John Jones." Also on the counter is his wallet, which has fallen open to show a bank card in the name of "Adolf Meyer."

John applies for employment, listing several out-of-town companies as former employers. The most recent employer, however, is closer than the others, and John lists the phone number of a friend who agreed to help him in this regard. If he gets a call to verify John's employment, he gives the caller a good reference. If this is the only call the prospective employer makes, this backstopping may work for John.

John applies for a government job. The application requires him to list all of his former employers. As he's never been employed under his new identity, checking with the former employers he lists won't produce any verification of his employment. John is not backstopped.

John happens to find a wallet containing I.D. for someone who bears an amazing resemblance to him. Overjoyed, he starts using this I.D., only to find that he now has a wife and six children in another state, and that he's liable for their support.

The Background Check

Employers, both government and private, are very aware of forged I.D. and assumed "personas." They know that people assume faked identities to cover up a criminal past or, in the case of espionage, to establish a "cover." This is why background checks exist.

Many years ago, checking an applicant's past was relatively simple, even for a government agency. It involved merely poring through the files for a criminal record, or for information that the subject may be an "undesirable." In the case of national security positions, a record of involvement with a subversive organization would be a disqualifier.

It was equally simple for an applicant to assume a new identity, leaving his past behind. A records check would produce no negative trace, and many slipped through this way.

This brought a new response from government and private employers. This new system was called "positive vetting" in Europe, where it was first devised. Instead of merely looking for "negatives," the personnel or security office now has to verify, or "vet," the applicant's existence and record "positively," by checking the background.

The procedure is simple in principle, but complicated in detail. The applicant has to fill out a form listing his entire background. This usually starts with date and place of birth, education, and employment history. It may also include listing every address where he has ever lived, and a number of friends and acquaintances. If the application is for a "sensitive" occupation, for the government or a defense contractor, it will require a "security clearance."

Security clearances vary in degree, from "Confidential" up to "Top Secret" and beyond. The higher clearances require more intensive investigations. A typical clearance, for example, requires filling out a multi-page questionnaire listing every job and every address. It also requires listing the names of all family members, their addresses, and places of birth.

The questionnaire is only the beginning. This provides a framework for a background investigation that can be very involved if the clearance is high enough. If, for example, the applicant is seeking work involving nuclear weapons or cryptosystems, he can expect the following:

- An investigator will contact everyone he lists who is still alive, to verify their existence and their relationship to the applicant. He'll also check them for criminal or subversive records.

- If he has foreign-born relatives, an investigator will check them out with the police of that country. He'll be interested in their criminal records, if any, and especially their political affiliations.

- An investigator will go to every address he lists as former residences, to verify that he actually lived there when he claims he did. He may also inquire about the applicant's character, asking neighbors whether he seems to have a drinking problem, beats his wife, etc. He'll also be checking out the mundane details, such as the applicant's wife's name and the number and ages of his children.

- His friends will be interviewed and asked how long they've known him, and what they think of him. Routinely, their names will be run through a computerized check for criminal and subversive records.

- All of the organizations in which he's ever listed himself as a member will get a once-over. An investigator will verify the applicant's membership and seek references about him. He'll also scrutinize the character of the organization, checking with various lists of subversive or suspect organizations.

- Investigators will also verify the applicant's school records in person, asking former teachers whether or not they remember him, and what they thought of him. There will also be a check of school yearbooks, especially those that have photographs, to compare with current photographs of the applicant.

- An investigator will also check the applicant's birth records. If he was born in a hospital that took fingerprints or footprints of newborn babies, the investigator will verify them against current ones to make sure that he is who he claims to be. He'll check details such as the names of the applicant's parents, as listed on hospital records and on his birth certificate. Some birth certificates list the infant's race, and he'll check that to see that it matches.

- An investigator will follow up on the applicant's medical records, verifying details such as blood type and scars from any surgery he may have had. He'll also check dental records, comparing fillings with current dental records.

- The applicant can also expect a check on his current family. Investigators will visit schools his children attend or have attended, to verify that they were actually there and to obtain impressions from any school officials who knew them.

- There will be verification of any foreign travel. Investigators will check travel records for any vacations claimed, to verify that the applicant actually went where he said he did. There will also be a check with foreign immigration and customs officials to verify his visits to those countries, and the length of stay.

The purpose of this intensive investigation is to show whether or not the applicant is the person he claims to be. The key is that there must be positive results from the investigation. It's not enough for the applicant to show up negative in checks of criminal files.

There have been instances of people taking over others' identities. In one instance, a Soviet spy assumed the identity of a man who became a Roman Catholic priest. In another, a Soviet spy assumed the identity of a Canadian who had been killed in the war. In both cases, the faked I.D.s worked, but only because the spies did not attempt to obtain employment for sensitive positions. They were eventually revealed by other means, not because their "cover" identities broke.

One tactic used by Soviet espionage agencies is to claim as background, institutions that have burned or disappeared. They collect instances in which a public records office was destroyed by fire, or companies that have gone bankrupt. This makes it impossible to disprove a claim based on these institutions. The system of positive vetting, however, deals with this problem by certification. Nobody gets a clearance without being positively certified by the investigating agency. An inconclusive investigation won't result in a clearance.

The final stage in a security investigation is an evaluation of the reports by a professional evaluator. The separate phases will have been conducted by many investigators because they will have involved many different areas. Because investigators typically conduct only their parts of the investigation as separate assignments, they don't know how each piece relates to the others. The evaluator reads all of the reports and tries to tie everything together. He'll look for gaps and discrepancies. If the applicant lists his mother's name as "Rosa" and his birth certificate lists it as "Maria," he may have to explain the discrepancy. If he stated that in 1959 he went to Switzerland on vacation, and the investigation shows a side-trip to East Germany, this will be a red flag to the evaluator.

If all of the details are verifiable, or the applicant can explain away minor discrepancies, the evaluator will pass him and award his "clearance." This is a certification that the applicant has passed the test and may have access to sensitive information.

The Pitfalls

From this you can see the problems involved when someone tries to make fake I.D. pass further than it's designed to go. There are definite limits to every level of illusion built into faked credentials.

The identity-changer needs to work his way around taking an identity that has built-in risks. A name similar to that of someone wanted for bad debts or child support will bring him more trouble than it's worth.

He also needs to know the limits of his credentials, or he will push them too far. In some cases, possession of forged I.D. is a crime. Faking official government paperwork is always a crime. However, forging a company I.D. card may not be, unless it is used for fraudulent purposes.

Necessary Steps

"Backstopping" is necessary for all but the lowest levels of fake I.D. One is a mailing address to support a bogus identity. Identity-changers use this because to order certain documents, such as passports, drivers licenses, or bank cards. A post office box is not acceptable as a mailing address. Only a street address will do.

One way people find such services is to look in the *Directory of U.S. Mail Drops,* published by Loompanics Unlimited. This provides a listing of mail drops that can be rented. For various reasons, people might not want to use a mail drop in their hometown, especially if it's a small town where everyone knows everyone else.

Mail drops or letter forwarding services can be hired in another city, state, or even another country without the user ever showing up in person. Money orders are the typical form of payment, and there are usually few questions asked.

Another way people find mail drops is through the classified sections of newspapers. Sleazy tabloids at the supermarket check-out usually have lots of mail drop ads. So do the mechanical and the "macho" mags.

At least half of these mail drops are totally useless for the identity-changer because they use a post office box instead of a street address. Others are somewhat undesirable because they use a "suite number" to disguise the box number that the mail drop service rents. Some mail drop operators take the time and trouble to sort mail by name. The exception is when people set up dummy companies, in which case the suite number is logical.

Informal mail drops are sometimes set up with the superintendent of a large building, residential or commercial. Because of the occupancy turnover in large buildings, the super is the person the postal carrier contacts regarding recent arrivals and departures. The postal carrier usually contacts the super regarding any mail he can't immediately place. Because supers are not the most highly-paid employees, they are often willing to undertake a few extra tasks, such as accepting mail for someone who doesn't rent at that address. A cover story, such as the need to protect assets from a gold-digging wife, is often employed to convince the super that nothing illegal is going on.

Supplemental Documentation

As we've seen from the library card incident described at the beginning of this chapter, showing the wrong I.D. can cause problems. The classic instance of running into a problem is the person who enters a country with one passport, and the customs inspector opens his luggage to find several other sets of I.D. It's at this point that the customs agent flashes a smile and asks the unfortunate traveler to step into a room at the side to clear up "a few formalities" that can take a few days to a few years.

Since it is dangerous to travel in foreign countries with two sets of I.D., spies and other people using fake identities often mail a second set of I.D. to themselves using a previously-arranged mail drop in that country.

Those who adopt a fake identity need a few things to support it, depending on how far they want to go with it. These auxiliary pieces of documentation are used as "props" to help carry out the role.[1] For example, business cards may be printed up cheaply and quickly.

A few other things usually carried in the wallet are a library card, various membership cards, and a "return if found" card. The return card is the easiest to fake, because most wallets come with one in a plastic pocket. Membership cards are the next easiest, because they don't have to be forged. Fifteen or twenty dollars will allow anyone to join many groups, such as the National Rifle Association, and obtain membership cards.

Various other cards come without asking. Insurance companies that use telephone directories as mailing lists send junk mail with various elaborately embossed insurance cards. These can be purchased in any name by answering ads in newspapers, magazines, and on the radio.

Simple Precautions

Backstopping is a simple precaution identity-changers use to avoid inconsistencies, which can lead to embarrassment and more serious problems.

Sources

1. *New I.D. In America,* Anonymous, Boulder, CO, Paladin Press, 1983, pp. 31-35.

5

What Goes Into Real I.D.

Before examining the techniques of the forger, we'll examine what genuine identity documents are like, and closely scrutinize the precautions taken to prevent forgeries. We can begin by laying out a few general rules:

- The older the document is, the less sophisticated are the precautions taken against forgery.

- The most recent documents, including bank cards and electronic I.D. cards, have very sophisticated safeguards that make it almost impossible for the would-be forger.

- Official (government-issued) I.D. is more difficult to forge than most privately-issued I.D.

- Security of any form of I.D. depends on using materials and techniques not commonly available.

There's a constant, see-saw struggle between the I.D. makers and the I.D. forgers, with each advance in document security soon outpaced by a quick and easy way to overcome it.

A Short History of I.D.

Early I.D. was simply a card or letter stating that the person was who he claimed to be, or that he was entitled to certain privileges. During ancient times and the "Middle Ages," this sufficed because few people knew how to read and write. A further safeguard was depositing a personal seal in wax upon the document. A king or nobleman had a seal, hand-engraved into a ring or a separate fixture, which he'd use to emboss in wax to authenticate his letters or decrees.

In ancient times, an engraved ring was
often used to seal documents to prevent forgery.

A person's signature was for a long time thought to be enough of an authenticator. This is because handwriting is very individualistic. However, forgery of handwriting is not an unusually difficult task, and a signature actually offers poor security.

Watermarks were another way to frustrate forgers. Paper would be passed through a press during manufacture, and rollers would emboss a watermark into the paper. This sets the paper apart from other paper of similar type without the watermark.

Another security measure is the fine pattern, printed in erasable ink, that is used to coat checks and stock certificates to prevent erasures and alterations. This process requires special inks which remain on the surface of the paper, and which come off or change color if there is any attempt to treat the paper with deletion fluid.

Patterns made with special inks that reveal alterations
or copying are often used in checks and stock certificates.

Indelible ink was another development preventing a forger from bleaching ink out with chlorine solution and inserting other writing in its place.

Proprietary card stock is another method used to frustrate forgers. This method uses a type of paper or card made to special order and unavailable on the open market. Forgers have always found restricted paper stocks easy to fake. Forgeries don't stand up to laboratory examination, but they pass casual scrutiny very well.

The most conspicuous example of proprietary stock is the paper on which U.S. currency is printed. This, also, is too easy to simulate, and counterfeiters have been passing bogus currency for many decades. The Treasury Department is planning a type of paper with metallic fibers for new currency.

The Nineteenth Century saw two outstanding developments which made document forgery much more difficult than the casual art it had been. One was the development of photography. It was now possible to paste a photograph onto a card, or to have personal details printed on the margins of a photograph. This made it impossible to simply pick up another's I.D. and claim it as one's own. The other was the recognition that fingerprints are unique identifiers. An I.D. card with a thumb-print in one corner is far more secure than a simple printed card.

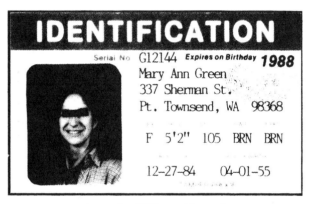

A standard I.D. card is made
more secure by adding a fingerprint.

Another technique used to enhance security was the use of a stamp across the photograph. This made replacing the photograph much more difficult because it became necessary not only to remove and replace the photograph without marring the paper, but to procure another seal and match the overlap exactly.

During the Twentieth Century, there were several other developments to make I.D. more secure. One was plastic lamination, to encase the I.D. card in a sealed plastic envelope that prevented alterations. It was obvious that a skilled forger could steam a photograph off a card or passport and substitute another. Lamination made this much more difficult.

The photographic I.D. card made cut-and-paste forgery impossible. Using a color negative-positive process, it's now possible to make an I.D. card that cannot be altered by cutting and pasting, without ruining the card. The one-piece construction prevents this. Unfortunately for the legitimate I.D. makers, photographic processes available to ordinary citizens make it possible to duplicate such cards and to fabricate forgeries.

Several simple manual systems were also devised to detect forgeries. One such, which was not designed as a security system but which can still trip up forgers, is the coding for place of issue of Social Security Cards. The first three digits denote the state of issue, and the number groups are distributed as follows:

Alabama	416-424	Missouri	486-500
Alaska	574	Montana	516-517
Arizona	526-527	Nebraska	505-508
Arkansas	429-432	Nevada	530
California	545-573	New Hampshire	001-003
Colorado	521-524	New Jersey	135-158
Connecticut	040-049	New Mexico	525, 585
Delaware	221-222	New York	050-134
District of		North Carolina	237-246
Columbia	577-579	North Dakota	501-502
Florida	261-267	Ohio	268-302
Georgia	252-260	Oklahoma	440-448
Hawaii	575-576	Oregon	540-544
Idaho	518-519	Pennsylvania	159-211
Illinois	318-361	Rhode Island	035-039
Indiana	303-317	South Carolina	247-251
Iowa	478-485	South Dakota	503-504
Kansas	509-515	Tennessee	408-415
Kentucky	400-407	Texas	449-467
Louisiana	433-439	Utah	528-529
Maine	004-007	Vermont	008-009
Maryland	212-220	Virginia	223-231
Massachusetts	010-034	Washington	531-539
Michigan	362-386	West Virginia	232-236
Minnesota	468-477	Wisconsin	387-399
Mississippi	425-428,587	Wyoming	520

These numbers are mostly formalities, especially because Americans move around so much. A person born in one state may attend school in another state and obtain his first job in a third or fourth state if his parents move a few times. Yet forgers can be caught using a Social Security number that obviously is not from the state from which it was supposedly issued.

Another number coding system, which has been in use for some time, is the "Soundex" System.[1] This is an alpha-numeric code grouping sound-a-like letters. The first character is the first letter of the last name. The next three non-doubled consonants in the last name form the next three digits according to the following code:

BFPV	1
CGJKQSXZ	2
DT	3
L	4
MN	5
R	6

The letters W, H, and Y have no number equivalents.

In Soundex, we can encode the name "Garcia" as G620. The "0" is used when there aren't enough consonants to fill the four spaces. Double letters, such as in "CaTTerson," are ignored.

This is the basic Soundex System. There are variants depending on the issuing agency. Using such a system enables a clerk or police officer to spot documents in which the numbers don't correspond to the sound of the names.

A coding system which is no longer in use, but which was designed to help employers who considered hiring former members of the military services, is the "SPN" (Separation Program Number) system. This used alphanumeric codes to denote the type of separation from the service the subject received. The number "201" meant that the term of service had expired. However, anyone discharged for bedwetting would get a number "263" stamped on his discharge papers. "249" meant homosexuality. "463" meant paranoid personality.

These codes enabled a prospective employer to discriminate between those who had served honorably in the armed forces and those who had been discharged for specific derogatory reasons.

These codes have not been used in military discharge papers since the 1970s, as a result of the Privacy Act.

Security Systems Today

Other coding systems are in common use. Some auto license plates are coded to match the area of the state in which they're issued. Drivers licenses may be coded in relation to the name or address. A simple way is to add the number "1" to each digit. For example, if the driver's address is 6801 12th. Street, his license number will start or end with "791223."

Bank cards have coded numbers, with the exact system depending on the bank. In most cases, the card numbers are linked to the expiration date. This is why, when ordering goods through a telephone 800-number, the operator always asks for both the card number and the expiration date. This provides an internal quick check for authenticity.

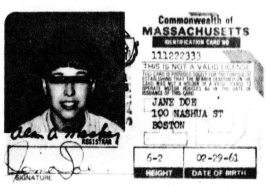

Superimposing a seal or signature over the edge
of the picture makes it difficult to substitute photos on an I.D. card.

Other methods used to enhance security involve "validation." Thus, a blank document is useless by itself. When properly issued by the agency or authority, it will have hidden seals or invisible ink codings. A signature or code number which remains invisible under normal light, but which fluoresces under ultraviolet light, is one way. This system provides two-level protection. Official document blanks are often vulnerable to theft. In some cases, they're handed out freely to applicants. Anyone applying for a drivers license will, for example, have to fill out a blank which later becomes the drivers license or which is photographed, along with the head-and-shoulders photo, to make the photo-I.D. The validation ensures that the document is genuine. Imprinting the state seal or the signature of the commissioner of the department on the edge of the photograph makes it more difficult to replace one photo with another.

U.S. Drivers Licenses

There are other kinks and tricks that motor vehicle departments use to hinder forgers. We'll go over them state by state:

Alabama:

This license is a photo I.D. card laminated in plastic. The driver's photograph is on the lower left corner, and overlapped by the state seal. The drivers license number and birth date are embossed at the top, and licenses of minors under 21 are further identified by a star embossed after the birth date.

Alaska:

This license is also a photo laminated type, but the lettering on it may be typewritten or "computer type," which offers the forger a choice. The signature of the Commissioner overlaps the photo. An additional safeguard is that the state seal overlaps the driver's signature.

Arizona:

This is a polyester photo I.D. card, but is not laminated. The state seal is on the front of the license, surrounded by a printed orange pattern which overlaps the type. The Assistant Director's signature is on the bottom. The driver's name, address, and other data may be typed or written in by hand.

Arkansas:

This is a laminated photo I.D., using the state seal overlapping the photo as a safeguard.

California:

This license is photographic, with a high-tech laminate on the front. Type may be typewritten or computer type. The state seal and the name "California" are hidden in the laminate.

Colorado:

This is photo-I.D. with a polycarbonate (Lexan) coating. This makes it very durable, as well as unusually flexible. The material gives it a different "feel" from most photographic materials. The state seal is in the center, and the Director's signature is in red.

The extra trick in this license is in the numbering system. The number begins with a letter for the year of issue, such as "G" for 1987. However, drivers under 18 have numbers with the letter "M" in front. Licensees from 18 to 21 have numbers beginning with "P."

Connecticut:

This is a Polaroid photo card, laminated in plastic with the gold printing "CONNECTICUT" on the plastic. A gold "Y" is in the typed area for minors' licenses. There are several other tricks and kinks to this license:

The Commissioner's signature is on the edge of the photo. The first two digits of the nine-digit license number are coded. For drivers born in odd years, the first two numbers denote the month of birth by the numbers 01-12. Those born in even years have the numbers 13-24 to denote the birth month.

Delaware:

This is also a photo I.D. with lamination. The safeguards are the Director's signature on the edge of the photo, the date and fee at the bottom, and a red background for the photos of those under age 21.

District of Columbia:

The D.C. issues photo-laminated I.D. with the Administrator's signature or the outline of the district map on the edge of the photo. The license number may be the Social Security number or one assigned by the issuing agency.

The trick in this license is the code number "3" in the space for "Restrictions" to identify minors under 18.

Florida:

This state issues photo-laminated I.D. with the state seal and camera number overlapping the photo. The license number follows the Soundex system and begins with the first letter of the last name and looks like this: J123-123-39-123. The two-digit group is the birth year. An additional trick is that minors under 21 have a yellow background on their photos. The most difficult to overcome trick used with this license is state seals printed in ink visible only under ultraviolet light.

Georgia:

This is a photographic laminated card with the blue state seal on the front, surrounded by a pattern of orange lines. The safeguards include both the Governor's and Commissioner's signatures, but not overlapping the photo. Drivers under 20 have a red bar at the top of the card.

Hawaii:

This looks more like a bank card than the typical drivers license because the data is embossed. The photo is at the upper right, embedded in the plastic card. An additional 10-digit number is at top right, above the photo, and minors under 17 are identified by having their photos in profile.

Idaho:

This license is a laminated Polaroid with a gold pattern in the lamination. Minors under 19 are identified by a photo in profile, instead of full-face. The license number may be the Social Security number. Otherwise, it's 9 digits beginning with "910" or "911." Only the Social Security number is hyphenated.

Illinois:

This is a laminated Polaroid photo-I.D. with the repetitive letters "ILLINOIS" on the laminate. This license is full of tricks.

As a start, the photo has a number overlapping it. The license number itself is coded. It begins with the first letter of the last name, followed by three digits coded on the last name. The next three digits are a code based on the first name and middle initial. The next two digits are the year of birth and the last three digits signify the person's sex, and the month and day of birth, again in code. The number is hyphenated in a misleading way, though: A123-4567-8901.

Indiana:

This is a photo-I.D. with a laminate on the front, which gives it a silky texture. There's nothing significant about the license number, which may be a Social Security or other number with 9 digits. One trick used in this license is listing both the expiration date and the date for re-examination. If they don't match, the license is fake. Additionally, there are state seals hidden in the plastic.

Iowa:

This is a photo-I.D. laminated in plastic. The tricks employed with this license are that the Director's signature and the station number overlap the photo. The license number may be the SS number or nine digits and letters. Minors under 19 have their photos in profile. An additional trick is the lettering "IOWA DEPARTMENT OF TRANSPORTATION" in the plastic.

Kansas:

This license is a laminated photo-I.D. with the state seal in front in the data area. Two signatures overlap the photo. There are a couple of tricks: Those under 21 have red backgrounds in the photos. The letters "KANSAS" are repeated on the laminate.

Kentucky:

Again, a photo-I.D. laminated in plastic. A camera number and signature are on the photo edges. A red band, saying "UNDER 21," identifies minors. A blue band with the same legend is in the plastic.

Louisiana:

This is a photo-I.D., laminated in plastic. The photo is at the right, with the state seal and camera number impinging on it. The tip-off regarding minors under 18 is the red background of the photo. The first two license digits are always "00."

Maine:

Maine has two licenses. The non-photo license is a large card, issued to senior citizens 65 and over. This one isn't laminated, and the validation trick is a date stamp on the left edge. The photo-I.D. is laminated and has two security checks: a state seal overlapping the photo, and the signature of the Secretary of State overlapping the top.

Maryland:

This is a plastic-enclosed photo-I.D. with a state seal across the data panel to make life tough for forgers. A repetition of the name

"MARYLAND" goes across the data panel, too. Minors under 18 are photographed in profile.

The numbering system is coded according to the Soundex system. The number begins with the first letter of the last name, and the following three numbers signify the Soundex code for the last name. The next three are for the first name, and the following two for the middle name or initial. The last three stand for the birthday and month.

Massachusetts:

This is like the Maine license, with the gold seal and state name appearing on the license. The security checks are overlapping of the photo by three items: the signature, camera number, and a small seal. All license numbers begin with the letter "S," and may be the SS number or other. Minors get a red heading on their licenses.

Michigan:

This is a photo-I.D. with a polyester finish. There is printing on the back for medical data or an anatomical gift. The security checks are a special laminate on the front. The numbering system is Soundex. The first digit is always a letter, corresponding to the first letter of the driver's last name. The next three are the Soundex-coded last name. The following three are for the first name, and the next three for the middle name. The last three digits are the birth day and month, again coded.

Minnesota:

This one looks spiffy, because it's a plastic card with embossed lettering and a photographic film overlaid with the photo at the right. There are several security checks to watch. The number is based on Soundex, and starts with the first letter of the surname. The next three digits are the name code. The rest are serial numbers. Minors under 19 have licenses with a black bar on top, and also the word "PROVISIONAL."

Mississippi:

This is the usual laminated photo-I.D. with the signature of the Commissioner on the photo. The seal overlaps the photo. Drivers under age 20 have the notation "MINOR" in red and the birth date is outlined in yellow.

Missouri:

This is a high-class photo I.D. which is flexible and not laminated. Security checks are the state seal and an orange pattern on the front of the license. The license number is Soundexed. The letter is the first letter of the surname. The next three digits are the coded last name. The rest are for the coded first name, the middle initial, and the month and day of birth, and finally, the sex.

Montana:

This is a normal-appearing photo-I.D. that is laminated, with a 45-degree profile photo of those under 19 and the usual full-face shot of adults. The security check is the expiration date stamped above the photo.

Nebraska:

This is a Polaroid photo-I.D. laminated in plastic. A signature is on the edge of the photo. Drivers under 21 now have blue photo backgrounds.

Nevada:

This is like the Nebraska license, but with the legend "NEVADA" stamped repetitively across the license. A signature overlaps the photo. Persons younger than 21 are photographed in profile.

New Hampshire:

This is like the Nevada license, but with the pattern "NEW HAMPSHIRE." There is a seal and a signature overlapping the right edge of the photo. The license lists both the Social Security number and the drivers license number. The license number is in code. The first two digits stand for the birth month. The next three letters are for the first and last letters of the surname, and the first letter of the given name. The next two numbers stand for the year of birth. The next two, for the day, and the last is to prevent duplication.

New Jersey:

This state issues both photo and printed card licenses. The cards are a snap to duplicate. The photo licenses are in plastic. The trick on both licenses is the number. The first letter is the first letter of the surname. Next, there are nine numbers representing the license number. Finally, the last five numbers stand for the month and year of birth, and the color of the eyes.

New Mexico:

This state issues photo-I.D. with laminated plastic. The plastic coating has "NEW MEXICO" printed over the face of the card. Minors get cards with the legend, "UNDER 21 YRS. OLD," stamped across the front.

New York:

New York is one of the last states to go to photo-I.D. The new license is a 3M photo card, with a reflective lamination on the face. This gives it a silky texture. The type is computer type, and the security check is the New York State seal printed on the surface. The license number is very long, with the first letter the same as that of the surname. The last two digits are always the birth year.

North Carolina:

This license is plastic-encased photo-I.D. with the legend "NORTH CAROLINA" repetitively stamped in gold. Licenses issued to those younger than 21 have blue backgrounds for the photos. A security check is the state seal at the edge of the photo. Another is that the spaces for the restriction codes and expiration dates are red-tinted.

North Dakota:

This state hands out plastic-encased photo-I.D. with the gold legend "NORTH DAKOTA" over the left panel. Security checks are the seal, signature, and camera number overlapping the photo.

Ohio:

This photo-I.D. may be laminated or plain. Drivers under 21 have their photos taken against a red background. The seal overlaps the photo, as a security check.

Oklahoma:

This is a fully-laminated photo-I.D. The security feature is the signature on the photo's edge.

Oregon:

This is a fully-laminated photo-I.D. with the camera number overlapping the edge of the photo. Minors get very special treatment in Oregon. Anyone under age 22 gets the legend "OREGON" across the data panel, and the notation, "Minor until:..."

Pennsylvania:

This is a fully-laminated photo-I.D. with the state legend and slogan across the top of the driver's photo. A strip on the right side of the photo contains the camera number. The notation "UNDER 21 UNTIL..." is on the top of under-age drivers' cards.

Rhode Island:

This photographic card is laminated. There is a "STATE OF RHODE ISLAND" legend printed repetitively on the data panel. Licenses for those under 18 have the word "MINOR" printed in the top bar. The license number is coded to the extent that the last two of the seven digits stand for the year of issue. A security check number and signature overlap the photo.

South Carolina:

This is a photo-I.D. with a protective coating. Both a signature and seal overlap the photo, but the license number isn't coded.

South Dakota:

This is a polyester photo-I.D. with a piece of plastic on the front. The security check is that the data is embossed on the card, like a plastic bank card.

Tennessee:

Tennessee issues both paper and photo-I.D. licenses. The photo-I.D. is laminated. The paper license uses two signatures for validation. The photo-I.D. has the seal and camera number overlapping the right edge of the photo. Drivers under age 20 are photographed in profile for the photo-I.D. card.

Texas:

Texas issues a laminated photo-I.D. with the seal and signature for validation. Drivers under 17 are photographed in 45-degree profile, instead of full-face.

Utah:

These licenses are photo-I.D. cards with lamination. A stamp of the letter "L" and a signature serve for validation, located on the left edge of the photo. The word "ADULT" is in the upper left corner of the photo on licenses issued to drivers over 21. Those under-age have the legend "UNDER 21" instead.

Vermont:

Vermont issues both a plastic license without a photo and a photo-I.D. The plain card has a green surface with white margins top and bottom. The photo-I.D. has a signature overlapping the bottom of the photo, and the type of license in green ink next to the photo. Adults have "OPERATOR" stamped, while minors under age 17 have the word "JUNIOR."

Virginia:

This state issues a two-part license. One part is green paper with computer type for the data. The photo-I.D. component is in a plastic envelope and has the state seal for a security check. The seal overlaps the upper right corner of the photo. The under-21 driver's photo is in profile.

Washington:

This state issues a laminated photo-I.D. The security check is the signature and legend "DEPARTMENT OF LICENSING" on the top of the photo. The state seal is to the left of the photo, and an orange state outline in the lower left corner of the card. Drivers under 21 are depicted in 45-degree profile, and under-18 drivers are identified by the letter "M" in the "Type" space.

The license number is heavily coded. The first five letters of the surname and the initials of the first two names make up the first seven spaces of the license number. The numbers stand for 100 minus the birth year, and additional codes.

West Virginia:

This photo-I.D. has the legend "WEST VIRGINIA" printed over the data panel. The state seal overlaps the upper right corner of the photo, and two signatures overlap it on the bottom edge.

Wisconsin:

Wisconsin issues both a plastic-encased photo-I.D. and a paper card, printed in purple. Either is valid. Minors under 21 have "PROBATIONARY" printed on the card, instead of "REGULAR." The security checks are a seal overlapping the right edge of the photo and the state seal overprinted on the data panel on the photo-I.D. The license number follows the Soundex system. The letter is the first letter of the surname, and the next three numbers are based on the Soundex of the surname. The next three numbers are from the given name and middle initial. The next two are the year of birth. The next three are the birth month and day, and sex, but in code. The last two digits are to distinguish numbers that otherwise would duplicate.

Wyoming:

Wyoming issues laminated photo-I.D. with minors shown in profile and the legend "MINOR UNDER 19" stamped on the card. Licenses are printed in computer type. A silhouette of a rodeo rider, and an orange pattern, are surprinted on the data panel. The signature of the Chairman of the Tax Commission is above the photo.

Canadian Drivers Licenses

Alberta:

Alberta issues a two-part license, consisting of both a paper card and a photo-I.D. The paper card has an elaborately-printed red border, with the information typed in. The signature of the registrar serves as a security check. The laminated photo-I.D. has a stamped number overlapping the upper right corner of the photo.

British Columbia:

This license is a laminated photo-I.D. with a signature and title overlapping the top edge of the photo. These licenses vary in color of the crest and building pictured on them.

Manitoba:

This is a bilingual, paper stock license, with a fold line between the two halves. A validation sticker serves as security check. The license number is alphanumeric, with the first five letters taken from the surname. The next group of two letters are the first and middle initials. Two numbers following are the results of 100 minus the year of birth.

Three final characters are coded digits and letters. Minors have "PROBATIONARY" marked on the license.

New Brunswick:

This province issues a bilingual, paper stock license in red, white, and blue. The security check is a printed signature, or a sticker with a printed signature.

Newfoundland:

This province issues a green-printed paper stock license printed in computer type. The banknote paper has a green printed pattern for security, to prevent alterations, and the second security check is the cash register printout.

Nova Scotia:

This province issues a green-printed paper stock license with an elaborate anti-alteration pattern, and printed in computer type. The security checks are the seal and signature. The license number follows the Soundex system, with the first five letters taken from the surname. The numbers following are from the day, month, and year of birth, with internal codes for the last two.

Ontario:

Ontario issues two-part licenses, one a card and the other a photo-I.D. There are two security checks on the photos. Both a number and the name "ONTARIO" overlap the photo edges. Another security check identifies minors. The birth date is coded into the license number.

The license number is alphanumeric, with the first letter corresponding to the surname's first letter. The next four digits are codes taken from the last name. The next five digits are the first name and middle initial, again coded. The next two stand for the birth year, and the last four are the month and day. An additional wrinkle is to add 50 to the number representing the birth month of a female.

Prince Edward Island:

P.E.I.'s license is a laminated Polaroid photo I.D. with a signature on the bottom edge of the photo. A security check for minors is the birth date included in the license number. The number is derived by coding the surname for the first four digits, listing the day, month, and birth year for the next six, without coding, and using the number "1" for males, and "2" for females, for the next digit. The last is a code digit.

Quebec:

Quebec issues a paper license in French. All security checks are in the numbers printed on the license. One security check is in the serial number of the license. Another is the license number itself, which is coded according to the Soundex System in this manner: The first letter is the first letter of the surname. The next four digits are Soundex codes for the surname and the given name. The next six digits signify the birth date, month, and year. The last two digits are internal codes.

Saskatchewan:

This province also issues a paper license, but in English. The security check is by a numbered sticker in the lower right-hand corner. An alternative security check is the printed legend "VALIDATED."

Miscellaneous

- Massachusetts has a state liquor control card which is a photo I.D. with the state seal and Registrar's signature overlapping the photo.

- New Mexico has a Twenty-First Birthday card, which is a laminated card with a space for the photo. This is issued by the Department of Alcoholic Beverage Control, and the information on it is typed.

- New Hampshire, Pennsylvania, and Vermont all issue cardboard cards with a space for the photo to be pasted and lines for identifying information. The PA card has the state seal overlapping the photo. All appear fairly primitive and easy to fake.

- A number of states issue "non-drivers licenses" because of demand. The drivers license has become so widely accepted as I.D. that even people who don't drive find it very inconvenient not to be able to present one when they cash checks or otherwise have to show I.D.

- Federal Alien Registration cards are now Photo-I.D.s. These have the person's photo on the left front, fingerprint on the right front, and printed identifying data on the back.

- Recent bank cards now have holographic seals. These are high-tech metal seals with a color image of the bank's symbol which appears to float in mid-air when viewed. When moved, it appears to change color, and to have three dimensions.

- Private company I.D. varies widely, because it has many purposes. Retail outlets sometimes identify their personnel only by means of distinctive smocks or uniforms, but this is more for the convenience of customers than for security. Retailers who don't want to buy their employees distinctive blazers or smocks will sometimes issue name tags. These may be made of cheap cardboard, or plastic, with the employee's given name on plastic tape. A plastic name tag will probably have the company name silk-screened on it.

  Some companies which have extensive dealings with the public may issue special identification to certain employees. The telephone company, for example, issues I.D. because repairmen often seek access to both businesses and private homes to repair equipment. Companies which rent, maintain, and repair business machines usually issue I.D. This is especially important in the case of companies which deal in mainframe computers.

  Any company large enough to own a mainframe computer keeps it in a specially-secured area, usually with its own air conditioning system, and with access limited to authorized employees. Because of the value of the computer, and of the information stored within, there's very strict control of who has access to it. Computer service personnel often have both special I.D. and are "cleared" by telephone before being allowed in.

- Armored car and courier companies also use high-security I.D., for obvious reasons. Large manufacturers with military contracts may have special I.D. This depends more on the size of the company than the level of secrecy. In a small company, there will be a "secret room" in which the classified work is done. This is always locked, and access allowed only to "cleared" personnel. Because the company is small, everyone knows everyone else, at least by sight. The limit seems to be about 200 employees; beyond this number, there's likely to be a system of badges in use.

Company I.D. badges are almost always plastic cards with a safety pin or clip on the back, designed to be worn all day while on company premises. These cards are either photographic cards or laminated photo I.D. cards, with the company logo printed on them. They also contain personal information, such as name, title, and department. Often, badges are color-coded, to denote authorization for access to different areas. There is often a hierarchy of colors, with only one or two colors allowed access to any area.

In theory, these badges provide absolute control, preventing access by unauthorized persons. In practice, even security guards are not always watchful. One engineer assigned to "top-secret" work pasted a half-tone photograph of Adolf Hitler on his badge and wore it to work for two weeks before anyone noticed.[2]

Magnetic Coding

Bank cards today have magnetic stripes on the back, which contain identifying information to allow automatic teller machines to "read" them. This common security system has other applications.

There are also magnetic locks, the first ones used around 1945, which use magnetically encoded cards as keys. The lock-box is a magnetic card reader, which cannot be "picked" as a conventional lock can. One well-known brand is Cardkey, which is so popular it has become a generic term.

*Modern bank cards have magnetic stripes on the back
that make them easier to use and harder to forge.*

A Cardkey has a magnetic stripe which a device inside the lock reads. If the code is correct, the door or gate unlocks. Some cards are laminated to hold not only the company logo, but a photograph of the bearer, and have a clip to allow wearing it while on the premises. This allows the Cardkey to serve as an I.D. badge.

For extra security, the system can use a "proximity" card reader. This system has no slot — the reader is behind a window pane. The user holds his card against the window and the device reads it, opening the door if the proper code is included.

Sophisticated Cardkey installations have a central computer which monitors use of each Cardkey. If one is reported lost or stolen, the computer can void it out, and anyone trying to use that Cardkey for access will find it won't work. If the central computer is monitored 24 hours a day by security guards, they can be alerted to respond if anyone tries to gain access by using a voided card.

Makers of electronic security systems, such as Cardkey, are using sophisticated computer techniques to prevent unauthorized access to secure areas.

A central computer also allows tighter security by eliminating "passback." It sometimes happens that a driver uses his card to gain access to a gate-controlled parking lot, then leaves his card in the slot or passes it back to allow another to enter. It's also happened that an employee has dropped his card out of a window to let someone else use it for access. The central computer monitors each use of the card, and when it senses that a certain card's been used for access, it voids it out for access until an "exit" is registered.

*An electronic lock "reads" the magnetic stripe from
an I.D. card to determine if access should be granted.*

The central computer also allows programming different cards for use for designated areas. This controls access without the need for a human guard to scan each badge for a color code. The system also controls the exits for the card bearer, allowing him exit only through designated doors. Another option is a sensor to sound an alarm if a door is open for longer than needed for an entry. Yet another option involves punching a code into a keypad after inserting the card. This allows use of a duress code.

Another capability allowed by the central computer is to log each Cardkey's use. This provides a permanent record of each access and exit and aids an investigation if any irregularity is discovered. It also allows access during designated time periods to certain classes of card-holders. Regular employees find that their cards won't operate doors after certain hours, while executives and security staff have unlimited access.

The coding security provided by magnetic card systems makes forgery very difficult. Conventional mechanical locks provide several tens of thousands of tumbler combinations. A magnetic coding system has millions of possible code combinations.

The cards themselves have undergone an evolution that's been mostly invisible to their users. The simple magnetic stripe seen on bank cards and many access control cards has been replaced by embedded magnetic materials.[3] These can be magnetic slugs, magnetic wires, and magnetic sandwiches. For additional security, the data contained can be encoded.

It takes a good deal of sophistication and equipment to forge a magnetic card. While it's possible to buy or improvise a magnetic reader, some cards aren't easily seen as magnetic cards because their elements are sandwiched or buried in the plastic.

The next step is the "smart card," a plastic card with one or two microprocessors embedded within. This technology, invented in France in the 1970s, may be the next widely-used step to prevent forgeries.

The microprocessor can be made practically fool-proof. Because it's a ROM, Read-Only-Memory, it's impossible to alter. The chip can hold a wealth of information about the client, which a teller machine or human interrogator can use to validate the card.

The Future

It's hard to predict which types of documents will be the most difficult to forge because of rapid progress in the field. Magnetically-read passports are a new program, but not so much for security as for quick list-checking.[4] Every port of entry has its passport control officers, who are often members of the immigration service or the security police. Every country has its proscription list, called the "watch list" in Britain and by other names in other countries. These are lists of individuals who are refused entry or surveiled when they do enter. The lists are now so large that they're cumbersome, and many suspects slip by the controls. Magnetically-imprinted passports make machine-reading possible, speeding up the formalities and enhancing accuracy.

As a rule, the federal government has the most money to spend, and can buy the most costly systems to enhance security. But money alone is not the answer. While federal high-security I.D. is almost fool-proof, many other forms of I.D. are much more susceptible to forgery.

Sources

1. *Changing Your Identity,* Anonymous, Conn Publishing, 1986, p. 34.

2. This was done by an acquaintance of the author's.

3. *Security World,* June, 1986, pp. 45-47.

4. *New Scientist,* January 5, 1984, pp. 9-14.

6

Obtaining
Simple Genuine I.D.

In some cases, genuine I.D. is so readily available that it's not worth the counterfeiter's trouble to forge it. One example is the bank card. Another is the checking account. We'll cover these in the appropriate chapter.

Social Security Card

Because this is a genuine U.S. Government document, many people are afraid to obtain one under false pretenses. Although this is the most useless of all I.D. cards, some people like to see them because of an exaggerated respect for anything printed by the U.S. Government.

The quick way counterfeiters get them without hassle is by mail. If they apply in person, they may have to explain why they are getting a Social Security card at such a late age, when so many citizens are now getting them in childhood or at birth.

There are only three explanations that make sense:

1) The person has been in a mental hospital since childhood.

2) The person has been in prison since childhood.

3)   The person has been out of the country since childhood.

It's easier to get it by mail. Applications are available at every Social Security office. These are free. Instead of filling it out there, the forger mails it in. The application requires two pieces of I.D. One is a birth certificate. The other can be anything with the applicant's name on it.

Membership Cards

These are surely the easiest form of I.D. to obtain. Like magazine subscriptions, most groups only require that you send dues. The cards are used as auxiliary identification, as explained in the chapter on backstopping.

To give you an idea of how easy it is to join various organizations, because they're so eager for support and money, about 25 years ago a Jew joined the American Nazi Party by mail. A few years later, a Black joined the Ku Klux Klan. In 1980, a Jew became the Secretary of the Arizona Chapter of the KKK.

Magazine Subscriptions

These are the easiest to get. Filling out a subscription card and checking the box that says, "Bill me later," gets the process underway. Magazines will be sent to whatever name is used when subscribing. There are no security clearances in the magazine subscription business. Payment can be by bill, and even a money order will be acceptable. All they want is money.

Diplomas

To prove his educational level, the forger might need a diploma or two. A quick way for him to get the genuine article is to look through college yearbooks until he finds someone with a name similar to his, or similar to the name he's decided to adopt. He then writes to the college's registrar, stating that his diploma and transcripts were destroyed by fire. He encloses a check for fifty dollars to cover the cost of new ones. He adds a note that says he'll be happy to pay any additional costs.

Quick Work

Although these forms of genuine I.D. won't get the counterfeiter very far, if he's seeking a basis for obtaining heavy paperwork, they'll serve to substantiate his bogus identity. If he's trying to establish a new persona, keeping the material that goes with it, such as magazine subscriptions, around the home helps bolster the image.

7

The Forger's Kit

Building a forgery kit requires know-how, time and patience. Successful forgery requires supplies which may not be conveniently available when needed. Furthermore, it may require some things which are no longer made, and which can be found only in second-hand stores or at garage sales.

Another impediment to the forger is encroachment from the law. It used to be possible to buy fake I.D. by mail. In 1982, the "False Identification Crime Control Act of 1982" came into law. It's now known as Sec. 2, Chapter 47, of Title 18, U.S. Code, and it prohibits selling fake I.D. by mail. Today, any sort of I.D. cards with the person's birth date on them sold by mail must have the legend "NOT A GOVERNMENT DOCUMENT" printed front and back.[1]

It's still possible for the forger to buy the various materials needed to produce fake I.D. This may change, though. Just as we've seen the passage of gun control laws which also encompass ammunition and components, including some spare parts, we might see strict laws controlling the graphics and printing industries in future years.

It can be expensive for the forger to acquire the tools and supplies he'll need. Yet, through careful shopping, forgers can obtain materials for much less than they'd have to pay if they were in a hurry and had to buy what was available at the time. What's more, some useful things are available for free.

Sources of Supplies

The forger can obtain most of what he needs through local outlets, unless he lives in a very small town. There are several appropriate classifications listed in almost every local yellow pages. "Artist's Supply" outlets carry small tools and brushes. X-Acto knives can be purchased at artists' supply shops or in hobby shops. "Stationers" and "Office Supply" outlets carry papers, cardboard, business forms, stamps, and much other material. "Printers" and "Typesetters" are listed under their own categories, but certain specialty items are harder to find. "Litho" film, for example, generally isn't available from "Photographic Supplies" stores. It is usually sold by "Graphic Art Supplies" or "Printing Supplies" stores.

Forgers often use blind checking accounts and mail drops for maximum security when purchasing supplies by mail. This is a safeguard against being traced through suspect purchases.

Papers

Forgers often stock different types of papers. One size in particular is most desirable: 8½" x 11" sheets. This size is standard for photocopiers. They're also a convenient size for forging diplomas and certificates, many of which are smaller. It is easier for the forger to trim an oversize piece of paper to match than it is to weld two smaller pieces to make a large one.

Many successful forgers work in the printing trades. It's easy for them to skim off a few from a pile of "run-up" sheets. Paper companies also give out sample stock books, containing one sheet each of everything they make.

Another way forgers acquire supplies is by attending printing conventions or trade shows. These are held at least once each year in the larger cities, and are usually advertised in the convention column of local newspapers. Graphic arts supply companies often give away tickets to trade shows, or tickets can be bought at the door. They usually run a couple of bucks.

Paper samples are available free from all kinds of vendors at such shows. Some ink companies give out samples of inks. Business form suppliers hand out samples of pre-printed purchase orders and warehouse receipts, needing only a company stamp to make them complete. Almost everything given out might be useful to the forger some day.

Forgers need to acquire old paper if they're going to make documents with any kind of credibility. There are ways of artificially "aging" paper, but the genuine article is so readily available that it's not worth the forger's bother. Old books, easily obtainable in second-hand shops or garage sales, usually have several blank fly-leaves. An important detail about this genuine old paper is that it usually has a higher rag content than modern papers, and this gives it a different feel.

Inks

The forger must have a stock of various types of inks to forge personal I.D. Ball-point pens were not used before about 1950,[2] and were not in very common use even then. There are a few stationery and art supply stores which carry the old-style liquid ink, and also the pens and nibs needed to use it. An alternative is the Fountain Pentel made in Japan. However, this writing instrument contains ink of modern formulation, which won't look exactly like old style inks.

Paints

A hobby shop is the source of supply for plastic modeler's paint. One brand is Testor's. The forger uses this paint to create or alter impressed plastic cards. Often, the raised letters have a contrasting color, and applying plastic modeler's paint with a fine brush restores the color when the card is re-embossed. A thin stripe of paint, applied with a number 000 brush, is used to fill in cut lines when a photo is replaced.

Photographic Aids

Fine artists' brushes are used to apply bleach and dyes to photostats. Many birth certificate copies are photostats, which is a process that was in wide use before xerographic copiers became popular. A photostat is a piece of thin photo paper with a negative image of the document on it. The background is black and the type and writing are white.

Altering these requires bleach for inserting new lettering and dyes for blanking out old writing. The bleach solution forgers use is sold in photographic supply shops under the name of Farmer's Reducer. It usually comes in two-part foil packets and is not expensive.

Dyes come in several trade names, one of which is Spotone. Spotone comes in at least six shades, and can be used straight, diluted, or mixed to match the exact shade of the photostat paper being altered.

Type

Without a printing press, or at least a typesetting machine, the forger will be handicapped in his efforts. There is, however, a way forgers produce professional-looking type with minimal cost and no equipment.

Art and graphic supply stores sell rub-on transfer type in several brands, such as Zipatone, Chartpak, Presstype, Formatt, and Letraset. These are plastic sheets that usually contain complete alphabets, with upper and lower case letters. The more comprehensive brands also have numerals and punctuation marks. The plastic sheet of letters is placed over the appropriate spot on a document, and the desired letter is rubbed over with the tip of a pencil or ball-point pen. The letter will rub off the plastic carrier sheet and onto the paper.

*Transfer lettering is available in a wide variety of
typestyles and sizes. A forger simply presses on the carrier
sheet with a pencil or pen, and the letters transfer to his document.*

Transfer lettering is available in many fonts (type styles) and sizes. It can be used for headlines, such as "CERTIFICATE OF BIRTH" and for body copy.

The same manufacturers also produce sheets of press-on artwork. One of the most comprehensive lines is sold under the Formatt trade name. Available are borders, logos, and assorted symbols and pieces of commercial art such as eagles, shields, circles and mortises, boxes, etc. These enable the forger to assemble the sort of impressive I.D. that looks professionally produced.

An important point about this sort of commercially-available artwork is that some of it resembles the kind found on official government documents. Although it's illegal to reproduce exactly the art found on currency and official I.D., it's not illegal to make look-alikes that can fool almost anybody.

Metal type fonts for use in a small hand press are obtainable from:

F & S Type Founders, Inc.
237 S Evergreen
Bensenville, IL 60106
Phone: (312) 766-1230

Wax

Wax is used in the forging of seals. The preferred type of hard wax is obtainable through a number of outlets. Local stationers may have it. Hobby shops almost always have it. Suppliers are listed in the yellow pages section devoted to candle-casting. The same outlets sell dyes used to color the wax to different shades.

Stamps & Seals

It's possible to make stamps from pieces of rubber and linoleum, using fragments of razor blades to shape the letters. Allied prisoners of war in Germany during World War II used this method to fake official German seals.[3] Hand-cutting rubber stamps is very time-consuming, and it's almost impossible for the forger to do a perfect job.

There are many types of gold seals available in any stationery store. These are the type found on diplomas. One problem for the forger is that these modern seals are self-adhesive. They are peeled off a backing sheet and stick to documents. The old style had to be licked to moisten the glue. These are scarce today, although they can sometimes be found at garage sales.

A gold seal printing machine is available from:

F & S Type Founders, Inc.
237 S Evergreen
Bensenville, IL 60106
Phone: (312) 766-1230

This machine requires a die and gold foil, also available from this supplier.

Various old stamps and seal embossing machines can be found at garage sales. Notarized documents require a notary's embosser. Retired notaries or their survivors often have these old tools for sale, usually for a very low price, a dollar or two. They can also be purchased retail.

Authentic looking seals and foils, along with the
embossers to use them, are readily available for purchase.

In many states, a notary's "seal" is actually two stamps. One is a rubber stamp giving the notary's name, the words "Subscribed and Sworn to me," with a space for the date, and a notation that says: "My commission expires..." The other is the embossed (raised) stamp, with the name of the notary and that of the state. The exact form varies from state to state.

One source who sells stamps and embossers is:

National Notary Association
23012 Ventura Blvd
PO Box 4625
Woodland Hills, CA 91364
Nationwide: (800) 423-5752
California: (800) 382-3604

Another source for notary seals, embossers, and supplies is:

Stationers Exchange
6819 Springhurst Street
San Antonio, TX 78249

This outlet sells seals and stamps, as well as a line of certificates. Notaries are authorized to perform marriage ceremonies in Maine, Florida, and South Carolina. This opens up other possibilities for the forger to create fake certificates. A blank for one state can, with a type change, serve for another state.

Rubber stamps are made in almost any type or style, and are usually available from local outlets. However, there is a source for the materials used in making rubber stamps:

Magic Systems
PO Box 23888
Tampa, FL 33623-3888

This is a national distributor of stamp-making machines and supplies. They offer five styles of type: Standard Cheltenham Bold, Script Type, Gothic, Italic, and Medieval. These are available in sizes from 8-point, which is somewhat smaller than standard book type size, up to 72-point, which gives letters almost ¾″ high. Magic Systems sells several sizes of starter kits, priced from $500 to $1,000 for the big operator. A book on making rubber stamps is free with each press kit.

Another source for stamp-making machines, supplies, and general printer's supplies is:

Jackson Rubber Stamp and Supply Company
Brownsville Road
Mount Vernon, IL 62864
Phone: (618) 242-1334
Toll-free: (800) 851-4945

They offer a free catalog upon request — a 20-page brochure which lists everything needed for making rubber stamps. The catalog is profusely illustrated to help customers understand some of the technical terms.

Some of the items listed are dating stamps, and kits for making rubber stamps. The lowest-priced press is listed at $440.00. An "Office Outfit," which allows assembling a rubber stamp of up to four lines from loose letters, costs $17.55. This allows the creation of inexpensive stamps for occasional use without any delay. This also allows modifying existing stamps by inserting type.

There are also logos available for use in rubber stamps. These range from company logos, such as "CITGO," to official-looking seals. An assortment of borders makes it all too easy for the forger to duplicate many certificates and diplomas.

Yet another source is:

Martin Rubber Stamp Supply
1432 Major Drive
Jefferson City, MO 65101

This company sells a rubber stamp press for $425.00, and an instruction book for $3.00. A catalog lists an assortment of supplies, such as moulds for various imprints. These include company logos and official-looking seals and mortises. The catalog includes nine pages of reproductions that can be used as "clip-art," or originals for reproduction.

Still another source for rubber-stamp machines is:

F & S Type Founders, Inc.
237 S Evergreen
Bensenville, IL 60106
Phone: (312) 766-1230

This company also has a comprehensive catalog of type fonts, which also can be used as clip-art.

Business Machines

Two types of business machines are often important to the forger. The first is an old manual typewriter. Nobody had electric typewriters in the old days, and the light and portable dot-matrix jobbies were not even a gleam in someone's eye in 1940. Manual typewriters are often obtainable at yard sales for ten or twenty dollars.

The other is the old manually-operated check writer. This is a device that embosses the amount of a check into the paper, and makes alteration almost impossible. This has limited use. Specifically, forgery of an old canceled check.

Photo I.D. Machines

There are many machines used in manufacturing photo I.D. that are commonly available for purchase. They vary in size, price, and ease of operation. Some of the more elaborate systems produce extremely secure photo I.D., and are correspondingly expensive.

Some produce a piece of photo I.D. that's a finished product. Others produce a card that has to be laminated before issue. One model has a laminator built in. Some use a Polaroid-type instant print material, while others use a negative-positive color film.

Some sources for photo I.D. machines are:

Allsafe Company, Inc.
PO Box 825
Buffalo, NY 14240

Caulastics
5955 Mission Street
Daly City, CA 94014

Commercial Security Service
Smithtown Executive Plaza
222 Middle Country Road, Suite 328
Smithtown, NY 11787

Datacode Systems
5122 St. Clair Avenue
Cleveland, OH 44103

Eastman Kodak Company
Instant Photography Division
343 State Street
Rochester, NY 14650

General Binding Corporation
One GBC Plaza
Northbrook, IL 60062

Identatronics, Inc.
425 Lively Boulevard
Elk Grove Village, IL 60007

Identicard
PO Box 5349C
Lancaster, PA 17601

Photokards
400 Riverside Avenue
Jacksonville, FL 32202

Polaroid Corporation
Cambridge, MA 02139

Stik/Strip Inc.
1911 Linwood
Oklahoma City, OK 73106

Printed Forms

Certain pre-printed forms are very useful to the forger. A good example is the baptismal certificate, which is still often accepted in lieu of a birth certificate when applying for official documents. They can be obtained at religious supply stores.[4] Buying one or two at a time from different stores over the years starts the aging process.

When buying printed forms, the forger must look them over very carefully. Many contain anachronisms, such as a date of printing. This is a give-away for those who try to forge documents that were supposedly issued many years ago.

There are several mail-order sources of supply for printed forms. Blank diplomas and degrees are available from the following:

Carroll Studios
PO Box 29001
Chicago, IL 60629

Ideal Studios
PO Box 41156
Chicago, IL 60641

National Certificate Company
210 Fifth Avenue
New York, NY 10010

Quality Products
PO Box 83053
Oklahoma City, OK 73148

Specialty Document Co.
PO Box 5684
El Monte, CA 91731

Union Cards

One way to get genuine "union cards" is to contact the National Craftsman Union at 210 Fifth Avenue, New York, NY 10010. They also sell a "Certificate of Journeymanship" in whichever trade the purchaser chooses.

Press Cards

Press credentials are available from:

City News Service
PO Box 39
Willow Springs, MO 65793

These won't work for any serious purpose. Many police departments issue their own press credentials to media people, and won't honor any others. Likewise, getting into the White House isn't as simple as flashing a press card. The Secret Service issues its own press cards, and only to correspondents whom it has investigated and cleared.

Military Documents

Some military certificates are obtainable from a couple of outlets. These are diplomas to certify membership in an elite corps or graduation from a special course. Suppliers are:

Military Graphics
PO Box 228
Dunkirk, MD 20754

RMD Graphics
PO Box 410
Bronx, NY 10460

Real Documents

For a forger to be successful, he must know what the real documents look like. The forger with foresight often takes long-term preparations. He saves any official documents he finds. If he finds an expired bank card in the street, he saves it. The holograph might come in handy. If a friend from another state shows the forger his drivers license, he tries to borrow it long enough to make a copy. If he has a Polaroid camera at home with a close-up attachment, he can shoot a quick pic of the license. Otherwise, he might find a coin-operated photocopying machine and run off a copy of each side.

The same for older documents, which are more valuable to the forger and easier to fake. He'll make photocopies of any real birth or baptismal certificates he finds. He can then use Liquid Paper to white-out the lettering and make a clean photocopy for his own use.

One of the easiest official documents for the forger to obtain and alter is a Federal Firearms License. Does this sound crazy? It's absolutely true. The Bureau of Alcohol, Tobacco, and Firearms (BATF) sends out Firearms Licenses only to dealers whom it has allegedly investigated and found to be free of criminal records. These forms are cheaply printed on the cheapest paper. Federal regulations require that the dealer keep the original and send a photocopy to each firearms supplier when he buys guns. The only requirement is that the dealer's signature on each copy be original. In other words, he can't sign his license and make copies. He must make copies and put his original signature on each one.

The forger could easily get a copy of an FFL from any dealer. He simply tells the dealer that he has a relative several states away who wants to ship a gun, but as he doesn't have a license, it's illegal. He asks the dealer to accept the shipment for him, offering a fee, of course. This will usually get him a copy of the license, supposedly to send to his "relative." It won't cost the forger a cent, either, because the dealer won't expect to collect his fee until he has the firearm ready to hand over. Once he has the license, the forger can white-out the dealer's name and address, insert whatever he wishes, and make as many copies as he likes.

It's cheaper and quicker for the counterfeiter to forge an FFL than to obtain one through channels. The BATF is a monstrous bureaucracy that works very slowly, and although nominally you can get licenses within 45 days after the application date, it can take many months. This is not because they're doing a careful job of checking people out, but simply because they are all on coffee break for weeks at a time.

One little-used way forgers get access to many pieces of genuine I.D. is by visiting the lost and found offices of large department stores claiming to have lost their wallets. The forger is accompanied by a friend who pretends not to know him. If the clerk brings out a box full of lost items, the forger pockets more than one wallet while the clerk's attention is diverted by the forger's friend.

Among the forger's most useful and easiest to obtain genuine supporting documents are business cards. For most Americans, the only way to avoid having people push their business cards at you is to commit suicide! Salesmen hand you their cards. Insurance adjusters hand them out. So do attorneys, doctors, and undertakers. In many offices, there's a stack of cards on the receptionist's desk for anyone who wants one or a few. With repeated visits to any business office, the forger soon has a short stack of cards of the same type, which he may one day put to use.

Collecting business cards doesn't bind the forger to the names printed on them. On the contrary, he can take such a card to a printer and order a batch printed with his name on them.

It's also common for forgers to attempt to collect business stationery. They may take a few sheets of letterhead from every place they have worked, in hopes they'll come in handy someday.

Letterheads don't have to be fresh and blank to be useful to a forger. Using only the top, with the company logo and address, and attaching a new letter, will serve for photocopies. An example of this is faking letters of recommendation when applying for a job. Stapling such a fake letter to a resume or application can help fill a gap in the forger's employment history and forestall a verifying telephone call.

It's easy for the forger to obtain letterheads from companies in another city or state. He simply writes them a letter on an innocuous subject which will provoke a reply. One way is to use one of his pre-printed letterheads listing a mail drop as a return address and apply for employment, stating that he has a Ph.D. in whatever field would be useful to that company.

He can do the same to obtain letterheads from government agencies such as the FBI, Secret Service, CIA, and even the NSA. Using them for photocopied forgeries will likely impress those he's trying to fool.

Preparing for the Future

Building a kit early saves the forger a lot of time and trouble when he finally needs it. Starting his preparations early lets him bide his time and obtain tools and supplies at his convenience and at the lowest possible cost. It also gives the forger time to practice and develop the skills he needs to turn out passable forgeries.

Sources

1. *I.D. For Sale In The Mail,* Michael Hoy, Port Townsend, WA, Loompanics Unlimited, 1987, pp. 5-9.

2. *Vanish! Disappearing through ID Acquisition,* Johnny Yount, Boulder, CO, Paladin Press, 1986, p. 33.

3. *Colditz: The Great Escapes,* Ron Baybutt, Boston, MA, Little, Brown & Company, 1982, pp. 62-69.

4. *Vanish!,* p. 32.

8

Forgery Techniques

Faking documents can be easy or hard, depending on what is being forged. Some documents are almost impossible to forge perfectly enough to pass. Others are easy.

A lot depends on how the forger intends to use the document. With rare exceptions, no forgeries will stand up to more than a casual examination. Even expertly-done forgeries are often detected by document examiners. A fake drivers license used when operating a vehicle is hazardous to the forger, because if a police officer checks it, the forgery probably won't pass. Using a drivers license as I.D. to establish a bank account or to obtain a library card is much easier, because the clerks who see it won't be subjecting it to a computerized search.

Successful forgers have taken the time to develop certain necessary skills. The most important is learning photography and its cousin, graphic arts. These skills are vital to those altering or creating many types of documents used today. Another skill is printing, or at least, knowing how to operate a small printing press such as an A.B. Dick Model 360. This will enable the forger to print letterheads and envelopes, and even make copies of many official documents.

Forgers often learn these skills at vocational high schools or junior colleges which have night courses for adults. Attending classes allows them to use equipment which is prohibitively expensive to buy, such as a process camera or printing press. They get "hands-on" experience in various graphic processes which they need to know if they are going to get into forgery deeply. It can't all be learned from a book.

The Basics

There are several methods used to produce forged documents. One is obtaining a blank genuine document and completing it in the forger's name. This can be very difficult if the document is a government document or a high-security private document. In many cases, however, the government gives forgers a head start by issuing the blanks. Drivers license applicants, for example, receive genuine forms which later become part of the drivers license.

Another method is using a look-alike. Forgers have surprising success with this method. How many people know what a baptismal certificate from St. Brigid's Roman Catholic Church in Brooklyn, New York, looks like? If the forger presents one of these to a motor vehicle clerk in California, how would the clerk know whether it's real or forged? To find out would require more of an investigation than the clerk's likely to undertake.

The third method used by forgers is to create their own documents from scratch. They can do this by altering and copying a real document, or by using a copy machine or camera to make up a totally new one.

Paste-Up

Paste-up refers to the assembly of the various parts of a forged document. Lack of paste-up skills often results in the forger making obvious errors. The fundamentals are very simple, but they need to be observed absolutely to make a passable document. Paste-up proficiency enables the forger to produce a document with lines that are evenly spaced and level. Hurrying in this step can result in a crude forgery with lines of type running "up-hill" or "down-hill."

Paste-up equipment used depends on the method of working. One simple technique is using a "grid sheet" and a light table. A light table can cost hundreds of dollars but, for the forger's purposes, all that is needed is a small plastic panel illuminated from the back, such as the type used to view color slides. A grid sheet is a piece of paper or card stock with ruled lines, which is placed under the document. By aligning the type with the lines, the forger can see through the paper and produce a document that looks professionally-produced.

Another common paste-up technique involves using a small drafting board and a T-square. The document is taped to the board, using the T-square to make sure it's straight. The T-square can then be used to align all of the type pasted onto the document.

The term "paste-up" can be misleading. It doesn't use old-fashioned starch paste, but rubber cement. The best form of adhesive, though, is wax. The waxing machine has rollers which deposit a thin, even coat of adhesive wax on the back of materials run through it. This allows sticking them to the document. Unlike cement, wax allows for the lifting and re-positioning of materials if they aren't put down properly the first time. A small hand-held roller, similar to the kind used to roll wall-paper, is used to press the waxed type down flat.

Without a drafting board and T-square, the forger can improvise with a right-angle drafting triangle. These are fairly inexpensive, costing two to five dollars, and they enable the forger to line the work up with the edge of a table.

In order to align materials better, forgers often rule their paper before starting. For this, they use a light blue pencil, in the shade known as "non-repro blue." This is a shade that doesn't reproduce in a copy machine or when making a litho negative.

Photocopies

The modern photocopying machine has made forgery extremely easy. The surprising aspect of this is that few people realize it. The government satisfies itself with the knowledge that a photocopier can't turn out passable copies of U.S. currency, and that drivers licenses don't reproduce adequately in a copier. Let's see what happens when a forger uses a copy machine to make forgeries:

Example: The forger wants a letter of recommendation from a former employer, although he never worked there. He solves it by bringing out a sheet of letterhead from his collection and typing a new piece of "body copy" on a separate sheet of paper. He then tapes the new body copy, which is a glowing testimonial to his abilities, to the letterhead and lays it on the glass of the copy machine.

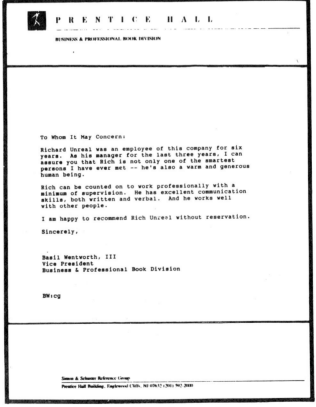

*The forger's first step in creating a made-to-order letter
of recommendation is to tape his text to the letterhead.*

The copy will have lines where two pieces of paper meet or overlap. These are called "paste-up marks" and are caused by shadows reproducing as lines. The forger eliminates them by going over his first photocopy with Liquid Paper to white-out the lines. Then he re-copies for a near-perfect forgery.

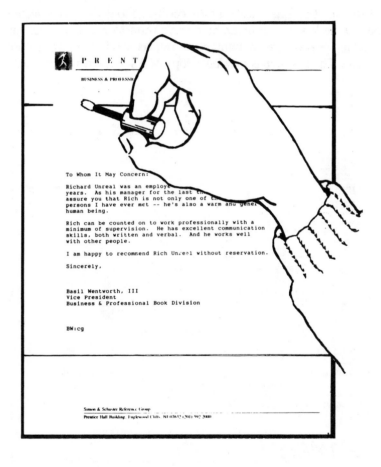

*The first photocopy of the letter will have
tell-tale "paste-up lines" on it. These must be
whited-out before a clean copy can be produced.*

A bold forger could even fake a letter of recommendation from the FBI using this method. This will raise some eyebrows when he applies for employment as a security guard. If he has a good story and looks the right age, he'll probably land the job.

Example: The forger needs a birth certificate to get a drivers license. The one he has is in a name he doesn't want to use. He solves this by taking advantage of human nature, as well as using a copy machine. The first step is making a copy of his real birth certificate.

This is a nice birth certificate, except the information needs to be adjusted. First, the forger makes a copy of the original.

He uses Liquid Paper to white-out the name and other details he wants to change. Then he makes a clean copy.

					Form approved Budget Bureau No. 68-R374.3.
STATE OF		**CERTIFICATE OF LIVE BIRTH**	**BIRTH NO.**		

1. PLACE OF BIRTH
a. COUNTY **WAYNE**

2. USUAL RESIDENCE OF MOTHER *(Where does mother live?)*
a. STATE **MICHIGAN** b. COUNTY **WAYNE**

b. CITY, TOWN, OR LOCATION **DETROIT**

c. CITY, TOWN, OR LOCATION **DETROIT**

c. NAME OF HOSPITAL OR INSTITUTION *(If not in hospital, give street address)* **HENRY FORD**

d STREET ADDRESS **1630 E. GRAND BOULEVARD**

d. IS PLACE OF BIRTH INSIDE CITY LIMITS? YES ☒ NO ☐

e. IS RESIDENCE INSIDE CITY LIMITS? YES ☒ NO ☐

f. IS RESIDENCE A FARM? YES ☐ NO ☒

3. NAME *(Type or print)* First — Middle — Last

4. SEX **M**

5a. THIS BIRTH SINGLE ☒ TWIN ☐ TRIPLET ☐

5b. IF TWIN OR TRIPLET, WAS CHILD BORN 1ST ☐ 2D ☐ 3D ☐

6. DATE OF BIRTH Month **06** Day **23** Year

7. NAME First **Robert** Middle **Allen** Last

8. COLOR OR RACE **Caucasian**

9. AGE *(At time of this birth)* **25** YEARS

10. BIRTHPLACE *(State or foreign country)* **Missouri**

11a. USUAL OCCUPATION **Executive**

11b. KIND OF BUSINESS OR INDUSTRY **Automobiles**

12. MAIDEN NAME First **Rosemary** Middle **Ellen** Last

13. COLOR OR RACE **Caucasian**

14. AGE *(At time of this birth)* **23** YEARS

15. BIRTHPLACE *(State or foreign country)* **Missouri**

16. PREVIOUS DELIVERIES TO MOTHER (DO NOT include this birth)
a. How many OTHER children are now living? **2**
b. How many OTHER children were born alive but are now dead? **none**
c. How many fetal deaths (fetuses born dead) at ANY time after conception? **none**

17. INFORMANT **Horace Greenfield, M.D.**

18. MOTHER'S MAILING ADDRESS **1630 E. Grand Boulevard, Detroit, Michigan 48109**

I hereby certify that this child was born alive on the date stated above. **18a. SIGNATURE**

18b. ATTENDANT AT BIRTH M.D. ☒ D.O. ☐ MIDWIFE ☐ OTHER *(Specify)*

18c. ADDRESS **Henry Ford Hospital, Detroit**

18d. DATE SIGNED **06/25/**

19. DATE RECD. BY LOCAL REG. **06/28/**

20. REGISTRAR'S SIGNATURE *Dena Rowlands*

21. DATE ON WHICH GIVEN NAME ADDED BY *(Registrar)*

FOR MEDICAL AND HEALTH USE ONLY *(This section MUST be filled out)*

22a. LENGTH OF PREGNANCY COMPLETED WEEKS **40**

22b. WEIGHT AT BIRTH **7** LB. **6** OZ.

23. LEGITIMATE YES ☒ NO ☐

(SPACE FOR ADDITION OF MEDICAL AND HEALTH ITEMS BY INDIVIDUAL STATES)

SAMPLE

Using the copy of the birth certificate, the forger white-outs the information he wants to change, such as name, date of birth, etc.

The forger then fills in any information he wishes, and makes another copy. He uses a notary stamp and embosser to give it an official seal, and takes it to the drivers license office. He tells the clerk that the original was falling apart, which is why he had a copy made and notarized. This may pass.

Example: A criminal wishes to order a firearm from out of state and have it delivered in a way that isn't traceable to him. He takes out a Federal Firearms License from his forger's kit. He makes a photocopy of it and whites-out the dealer's name.

The most common type of license is "Class 1- Dealer in Firearms other than destructive devices or ammunition for other than destructive devices." This means all ordinary pistols, rifles, and shotguns. It does not include automatic weapons (machine guns) or rocket launchers, and other "Rambo" type material.

Other classes of licenses are Classes 2 to 7. Class 3 deals in Fully Automatic Weapons. Class 7 is for a Manufacturer of Firearms other than Destructive Devices.

If this criminal took the license from a Class 1 dealer, and he wants to use it only to get Class 1 weapons, he leaves it alone except for changing the name and address, substituting his alias and mail drop address. The mail drop address can never be a post office box because, by law, dealers cannot ship through the U.S. mail and the post office will not receive packages from other carriers.

Before setting out to produce the new license, the forger checks a few important details, just to cover all of the bases. The license should have an expiration date on it. If the license is not yet expired, he's in the clear. If it is, he'll change the expiration date.

The license also has a number.[1] The numbering system used produces a long and complex number that looks like this: 9-86-013-01-C8-11032.

The first digit, 9, is for the administrative region. The second and third, 86, stand for the IRS district. The next three digits stand for the county of the state. The forger won't have to worry about this if the dealer's location is near his mail drop.

The next two digits, 01, stand for the class of license. This is an important point, because it must correspond with the entry in the "Type of License" box. If the forger decides to change it to Class 3, to order automatic weapons, he must also change this to match.

The next two digits are a letter and a number, in this case "C8." This stands for the expiration date, March, 1988. "C" is the third letter of the alphabet and March is the third month of the year. "8" is the last digit of the year the license expires. This is the second critical point the forger must consider. If the license is already expired, he'll have to change it, and re-work the number to match. Let's say he wants the new expiration date to be December, 1993. The correct two-character set to insert would be "L3."

The last five digit number is the licensee's individual serial number.

To have the firearm shipped, therefore, the forger sends in his order, payment, and a signed copy of the re-worked FFL. As long as it hasn't expired, and it's the correct class for the type of weapon he ordered, the order likely will go through. Firearms manufacturers and distributors don't scrutinize license forms with magnifying glasses. They file them away simply to cover themselves and ship the weapons ordered.

Example: A forger would like to have some auxiliary documentation for support when he applies for a job. His solution is to fake a document that is perfect for faking: a newspaper article. He selects an article that tells about someone he'd like to be. For example, "Noted Businessman Wins Man of the Year Award." He carefully cuts it out from the newspaper, substitutes his name and photograph, and makes several photocopies. He'll need to have his name typeset in the same typeface as in the article. For his photograph, he'll need a screened print. See the section on professional help.

There are several sources for originals forgers can use for making photocopy forgeries. One, of course, is a copy of a genuine document. Other sources are the documents provided in several books.

One such book is *Become Someone Else!,* by Nu-Way Publishing, no address listed. This has examples of seals and embossings on Page 9. Two versions of birth certificates are on Pages 30 and 31.

Document Preparation, by The Technology Group, P.O. Box 93124, Pasadena, CA 91109, has several generic I.D. cards on Pages 30 and 31. An appendix, starting on Page 35, contains baptismal certificates from several different denominations, birth certificates from several jurisdictions, and marriage certificates. There are also several types of I.D. cards, such as Minister's Identification, a Divorce Judgment, and type in various sizes for insertion into documents.

Forgers must take some precautions when using this book. Some of the type is "filled in," from too much copying. There are some misspellings, such as "IMMAGRATION OFFICER" on Page 72. This spelling might fool an illegal immigrant unfamiliar with English, but not an immigration officer. All of the type shown is produced with a dot matrix printer, and shows the ragged edges characteristic of this sort of printing. This is especially visible on the larger type sizes, and totally useless for forged documents.

Eden Press, P.O. Box 8410, Fountain Valley, CA 92708, puts out a source book for quick copying of typed legends. Page 44 has an assortment of half-tone reproductions of seals and embossed stampings. These are suitable for crude documents, but not for anything that has to pass a public official. Photocopying machines don't produce half-tones selectively, and this will scream "FORGERY" to anyone who knows this or who is accustomed to seeing copies of the real things. Pages 45, 46, and 48 have an assortment of legends, such as "Bureau of Vital Records," "Notarized," and "Valid When Signed By Registrar." There are also state and Canadian province names, and titles of offices such as "Department of Transportation." An assortment of numbers allows for reproduction on forgeries.

There is a small assortment of state seals on Page 15 of *How Drivers Licenses Are Made With The Polaroid Camera,* by Carl Dorski. A better reproduction of state seals is on Page 17 of a manual of the same name published by The Reliance Group, no street address listed, Stockton, California.

Another source for state seals is the state's own letterhead and other publications. One way a forger obtains these is by writing to the state's tourist bureau. This will result in receiving a letter in reply, several maps and tour guides, and other publications. One or more of these will have the state seal.

Watermarks

One way of forging a watermark involves obtaining a stamp of the design and using a solution of "water glass." This also goes under the generic chemical name of "sodium silicate." The sodium silicate solution makes the paper translucent, and gives the visual appearance of a watermark.

Many watermarks are crude, and it's possible to forge a stamp by cutting a potato or piece of rubber. For one-time use a potato is much easier to cut.[2]

Signatures

Signatures don't usually present a problem for the forger altering or copying a document, because any necessary signatures are already on the paper or card. When creating a document from scratch, the forger will often have to forge a signature. There are several ways he does this.

One is inventing a totally false signature. This will work if he's trying to pass a document from out of town or out of state, because the person whom he has to fool will almost certainly not know the real person's name. This is especially applicable to birth and baptismal certificates. Drivers licenses are another story. In some cases, the person he's trying to fool may have recently seen a license from that state, and may remember the signature.

Copying the signature, using pen and ink, or a fine brush and Spotone for photo-I.D. cards, is another method used. In this sort of forgery, it's more important for the forger to use firm strokes than to get the handwriting copied perfectly, because a common tip-off to a forged signature is shaky hand-writing. If he has to alter a drivers license or other document which has his signature on it, he'll probably re-do the document to include the name in his own handwriting. This is because some situations may require him to sign his name in front of a clerk, and any hesitation or display of shaky hand-writing will suggest that he's uncomfortable with the signature.

Yet another way to forge a signature is copying it from a real document using litho film, and over-printing it on the copy of the forged document. There are several ways of doing this.

If the document is to be a photo-I.D., making a second exposure on the blank copy will work. If the document is plain paper, making a rubber stamp of the signature will produce a passable copy. Neither method will look like an original signature, but the original documents also carry only reproductions. A commissioner of transportation does not spend his day signing drivers licenses.

If the signature must be a one-time copy, to authenticate a document, tracing is the most common method. The forger places the original on a light table, places the copy on top of it, and traces the signature. Practice tracing on blank paper avoids the risk of spoiling the work.

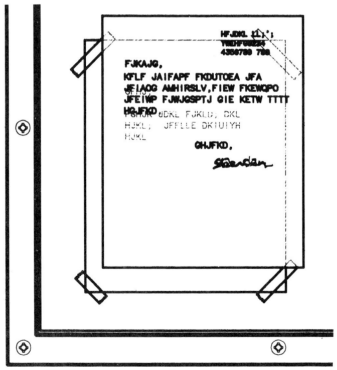

The best way to accurately copy a signature is
to tape the original document to a light table, then
tape the copy in position over it, and trace the signature.

In faking signatures, the forger must be aware that while it's hard even for a documents examiner to prove conclusively that a good forgery is indeed faked, there are some obvious errors that tip off the authorities. One is using a copy where an original signature is required. If the document being forged will get close examination, the paper fibers must be disturbed, just as the strokes of a pen disturb them. A rubber stamp won't do that, nor will a photocopy. Another error is using the wrong pen or ink. This is especially true for old documents.

Touching-up a signature on a photo-I.D. is tricky in this regard. This happens when it's necessary to have the signature overlapping the photo. Using a regular ball-point won't do at all, because the ball will indent the paper. A metal or plastic ink pen will probably produce a very poor result because it can scratch the surface of the photo paper. The ink, too, is totally wrong, and may produce a "dichroic" image: it appears black when viewed directly, but changes color when viewed at an angle. Finally, the ink may simply be the wrong shade of black.

The safest way for the forger to copy or touch up a signature on photo-I.D. is by using spotting colors, and mixing them to match the shade of the type on the paper. Applying the spotting dye requires a fine brush, which won't abrade the surface.

Genuine Fakes

In some instances, it's unnecessary for a forger to alter a real document. It's just as easy for him to create his own. An example is applying for a library card. In the past, all that was required was something with your name and address on it. An envelope with a local address on it would do. Today, most libraries require a drivers license or some similar piece of I.D. But if the forger claims to have left his wallet at home, he might be able to get away with showing an envelope addressed to his alias at a local mail drop.

Another way of making this sort of informal I.D. pass is by creating a letter, on the letterhead of a local company, offering the recipient a job. It's addressed to his mail drop, and he explains that he's recently arrived in town and is staying with a friend.

Another form of genuine fake I.D. is the plastic I.D. card service that some office supply stores offer. These will take a person's photo with a special camera that places his head and shoulders in a corner of an I.D. card that he makes up. They can be made with the heading and logo of an imaginary business, such as "Acme Hijackers, Inc.," and then used as an instant "employee identification" card. This can serve for check-cashing.

Altering Photostats

Many birth certificates are actually not certificates at all, but extracts from municipal birth records. These may be original documents or photostats. In other cases, the original birth certificate stays on file with the city or county record office, and the individual can buy a photocopy of it. Before copying machines became common, all that was available was the photostat.

Example: Altering a photostat to show an earlier date of birth. This can help the forger obtain a drivers license, for example.

For this, he will need several photostats, not necessarily all his own. The spares are used for practice. He also needs a very fine number 000 camel hair brush and some Farmer's Reducer. He'll also need some Spotone retouching dyes.

The year of birth is altered on a photostat of a birth certificate.

Let's say that the forger has a birth date of January 1, 1969, and he wants to show that he was born in 1961. The simplest way for him to modify the photostat is to fill in the loop of the "9" with Spotone and make it look like a "1."

In applying the Spotone, there are two important points for him to watch. The first is to match the tone of the paper. There are warm (brownish) blacks and cold (bluish) blacks, and Spotone comes in several shades to allow mixing to match. If he uses a tone that's noticeably warmer or colder than the photostat he's altering, his handiwork will stand out.

The other point is that he must use a dilute solution and apply it in stages. If he uses the concentrate it will leave a stain that's darker than the photostat. That, too, will stand out as an obvious alteration.

Let's see how the Farmer's Reducer might be used to bleach parts of the image. Let's assume that the January 1 birthdate isn't right, and he wants to make it January 11. If there's room, he can insert a second "1."

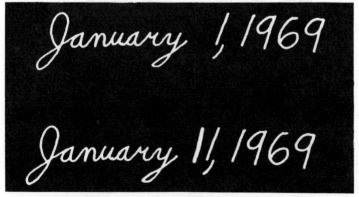

The date of birth is altered on a photostat of a birth certificate.

There are some fine points for the forger to watch when using a reducer on any sort of photographic paper. First, Farmer's Reducer is only a trade name. If unavailable in local photography stores, the chemicals can be ordered by their generic names. The orange crystals are potassium ferricyanide. This chemical isn't terribly poisonous, unless eaten by the spoonful. This is simply a bleach for the photographic image.

It must be mixed to make a medium yellow solution, with the crystals completely dissolved. The solution must be weak enough so that one application doesn't bleach the image. If it's too strong, there is a risk of staining the paper yellow. This stain may never come out.

With the fine brush, the forger applies the solution as if writing the number "1" in the same hand as the other numeral "1" on the birth certificate. He then let's it dry.

The "fix" solution can be any photographic fixer. This might be pure sodium thiosulphate crystals, or a liquid "rapid fix." They all work similarly for this purpose. A dilute solution is mixed — no more than half normal strength as in the directions on the package.

A slight amount of fixer is applied with a cotton swab. This enhances the bleaching action and removes any yellow coloring.

To alter a photostat, the forger uses a bleach solution to make changes, followed by a "fixing" solution applied with a cotton swab.

If this doesn't work, the forger can try again with the yellow reducer fluid. It is applied lightly, allowed to dry, then is followed with the fixer. The forger must be patient, because the document can be spoiled by hurrying. The fixing solution is rinsed off with a few drops of water when finished.

Another way forgers alter photostats is more elaborate, and requires a process camera and a darkroom. It also requires knowledge of graphic darkroom procedures.

The forger starts by making a negative of the photostat on high-contrast "litho" film, and makes a negative of the alteration he wants to insert. On a light table, he "strips" them in register, masks out the parts he wants to delete, and registers his insert on top of it. This gives him two negatives, which he attaches to stripping tabs to allow a double-exposure in register. Using a piece of thin photographic paper similar in consistency to photostat paper, he tapes it down in a contact frame, tapes the register pins to position one of the negatives over it, and makes an exposure. He then removes that negative, places the other in position, and makes a second exposure. He then processes the paper and has a genuine altered document, with no evidence that it has been altered.

It's possible for the forger to make many alterations with litho negatives. One common technique is masking by "opaquing" out unwanted lines. This means using a brush to apply a dense red paste, called "opaque," to the negative to block the light from areas that shouldn't be printed. Opaque is usually used to touch up a negative by blanking out dust marks and "pin-holes." For lines of type or writing, using litho tape may be more convenient. This is transparent red tape that blocks everything but red light from passing through the negative. Litho negatives and papers are not sensitive to red light.

Anachronisms

There's a real danger to the forger of giving himself away by neglecting certain small details. If he's creating a document that dates from many years ago, he might use two-letter state abbreviations such as "CA," and "MD" in the address. These didn't exist back then. Zip codes didn't, either. Telephone area codes have been around only since about 1960.

Another such detail is ink. Modern inks didn't exist years ago, and if a document is supposed to be several decades old, the inks must look somewhat faded.

Aging the Document

Most documents forgers need will have to be fairly fresh, so aging isn't much of an issue. In the case of birth or baptismal certificates, it may be necessary for the forger to "age" them artificially. There are several procedures for artificially aging a document. The simplest is baking it in an oven at about 300 degrees for 20 minutes.[3]

Another way gives the paper an aged and brown tint by immersing it in diluted coffee for a few seconds. The forger usually does this before writing on it, because the old types of ink run. After the coffee bath, the paper is hung to dry for a few minutes. A quicker method involves placing the paper between two sheets of blotter paper and using a hot iron to force-dry it.

Coffee has a distinctive odor, which lingers on the paper for some days. An alternative way of producing the aged look is by immersing it in tea, which also stains it but doesn't have the characteristic odor.

A quick way used to give a document a dirty, aged, and worn appearance is rubbing it with dirt. The document is folded over a few times with dirt in the folds, and pounded to grind dirt into the fibers. Particles of dirt are shaken free from the document, which is then dried.

Getting ink to fade takes longer. One way used is leaving the paper in the sun for a few days. Another way is baking the document.

Yet another way forgers try to make a document such as a birth certificate look old and "grungy" is folding it up and keeping it in their shoe for a day or two. The combination of walking on it and the absorption of sweat will age it very quickly. It will also have an aged smell that will discourage close examination.

Ultra-Violet Inks

These inks are commonly available. "Head shops" often stock them, because of the demand for psychedelic effects.[4] So do some printing supply companies.

Excessive Reproduction

The forger must avoid excessive reproduction of a document or piece of artwork to retain quality. This is often a stumbling-block for the beginner. We'll discuss briefly the theory of graphic reproduction to lay out the basics.

Every document begins with what is called "original art." This may be a card, letter, drawing, or other paper depiction of something, whether it be writing, printing, or an official seal. There are several ways of copying the original. Some of these, such as offset printing, are used in the original production of legitimate documents, such as birth certificates. Each reproduction of a document or piece of art, by whatever means, is called a "generation." Depending on the art, the method, and the skill of the operator, a certain amount of quality loss occurs with each generation. Let's look at the letter "W," for example:

Excessively reproducing a document will cause the letters to fill-in.

We see on the left the original printed "W," which is crisp and clear. The "W" on the right has been reproduced too many times, and we see the inside corners rounding and the spaces filling in. With other typefaces, such as Bodoni, the thin lines at the tops and bottoms of letters will drop out.

We see the original "C," set in Bodoni type, on the left. Too many generations cause the thin lines at the top and bottom of the "C" to vanish. This can also happen in one generation if the operator over-exposes it.

*Too many generations of printing or
copying will also cause thin lines to disappear.*

*Specially designed "security" typefaces use a combination
of very thin lines and very thick lines to make copying more difficult.*

Generally, the smaller the type the more difficult it is to reproduce it. The lines are finer, and tend to drop more quickly. There are also "security" typefaces which are truly nonreproducible, but these are rare. Usually, efforts to defeat reproduction use typefaces that include both very fine lines and very fine spaces in the typeface.

We see that there are very fine lines in the letter "m," as well as very thin spaces between the vertical lines. To reproduce the fine lines, it's necessary to cut the exposure to "hold" them. This causes the thin vertical spaces to fill in. Giving more exposure to hold the spaces will result in "burning out" the fine lines.

These "non-repro" typefaces are used only in very high-security I.D. and other documents. They're totally unsuitable for mass production, as in drivers licenses and other ordinary I.D.

We find that excessive reproduction also works against the forger with photo-I.D. Each reproduction results in more blurring of fine detail and a shift in color balance. While the quality of reproduction of most drivers licenses is low, allowing some latitude for the forger, he still needs to produce a forgery that looks enough like a genuine license to pass.

Now that we've covered paper documents, let's see how forgers handle more elaborate ones, such as plastic cards and photo I.D. The next chapter will cover these.

Sources

1. *Federal Firearms Regulations,* published by the Department of the Treasury, Bureau of Alcohol, Tobacco, and Firearms, 1985-86, p. 73.

2. *The Black Bag Owner's Manual, Part Three: False Face,* Boulder, CO, Paladin Press, 1979, p. 18.

3. *Vanish! Disappearing through ID Acquisition,* Johnny Yount, Boulder, CO, Paladin Press, 1986, p. 37.

4. *Black Bag Owner's Manual,* p. 20.

9

How Bank Cards
And Photo I.D. are Forged

Bank Cards

Bank cards are easy to forge, except for the magnetic stripe. This limits the possible uses. Criminals who try to use bank cards to operate automatic teller machines find that they need to key in a Personal Identification Number, or "PIN," to gain access to the account. The few instances in which there have been successful thefts this way have involved kidnaping the victim and coercing him or her to punch in the PIN at the machine.

Using bank cards for backup I.D. is much more common. This greatly lessens the chances of close examination and detection.[1] There are several methods used to produce faked cards.

One is altering a real one. An old card, discarded because of expiration, can still serve as backup I.D. because unless it's used for a cash transaction, people usually don't look at the expiration date. Another way is flattening the embossed date and re-embossing it. Flattening is done by applying heat.

There are two common ways of heating a bank card: totally and locally. Total heating involves immersing the card in hot water until the plastic resumes its flat shape.[2] Local heating is done with a soldering iron or a steam iron, depending on the size of the area being flattened. An embossing machine, available through stationery and office supply outlets, is used to replace the letters and numbers that were flattened.

A source for embossing machines is:

Perma Products
275 NE 166th Street
North Miami Beach, FL 33162

The embossed letters usually have a black tint which contrasts with the light background of the card. Forgers often touch up the new raised letters with plastic modeler's paint, available in most hobby shops.

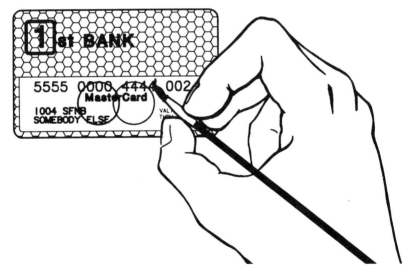

Touching up the raised numbers on an altered credit card.

The signature panel on the back of the card can be a problem for forgers. They might luck out and find a card that the owner forgot to sign. Usually, the signature panel has a security pattern printed on it. This is designed to show erasures. One technique used by forgers to replace a signature is to mask around the panel with masking tape and then spray the back of the card with flat white spray paint to cover the signature.

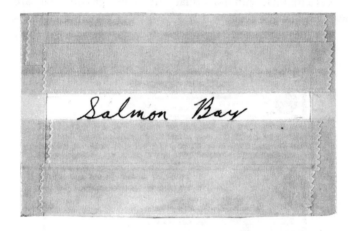

By taping over, or "masking," everything but the signature block, the back of an I.D. card may now be spray painted with white paint. A new signature is added when the paint dries.

The paint will also cover the security pattern, but this may not be noticed. It won't pass in a bank, of course, if the forger is trying to withdraw money from an account. But as supporting I.D. when opening a bank account or cashing a check, it usually doesn't have to be taken out of the holder.

Recycling old cards requires the forger to first procure them. This is a chancy process, and going through dumpsters is a time-consuming operation. One ring of forgers devised a far more efficient method in 1983. They robbed the company that manufactured VISA card blanks and obtained over 6,000 of the genuine articles.

Another way forgers get these cards is to manufacture them from scratch. Flat white plastic sheet is available from plastic supply houses, listed under "Plastics" in the Yellow Pages. Forgers then silk-screen the required logos and type lines to produce a card that serves as raw material for a basic-level forgery. An embossing machine does the rest.

Cards made this way are susceptible to scratching, especially if carried loose or with other cards in a wallet. Protection is provided by the card divider, with individual vinyl envelopes for each card, that comes with many wallets.

Photo I.D.

A Firearms Control Board Registration is a fairly easy piece of supporting I.D. to acquire and forge.

While some types of photo I.D. can be obtained fairly easily and cheaply, as we've discussed elsewhere, in some instances forgers attempt to make their own. Let's first consider the forgery or alteration of early-generation photo-I.D., as in the case of this New York City Firearms Control Board Registration.

In original form, this is an 8½″ x 11″ sheet of white paper, printed in black ink, and with the individual information filled out in blue pen. The city seal is in the upper left-hand corner, along with the union "bug" in the top line. Validation is by serial number and date stamp in the upper right-hand corner. The individual's black and white photograph is firmly taped on with two overlapping pieces of tape. A couple of slashes across the last three spaces for listing firearms supposedly prevents listing other weapons after the paperwork is issued. An additional security check is the space above the list panel for "TOTAL GUNS."

Forging this is easy for someone with the desire and a little know-how. The simplest way is to go to the Firearms Control Board and ask for an application. This results in a blank form. Filling it out, and stamping a reproduction of the "validation" with an office stamp kit gives it authenticity. Taping a photograph in place completes the form.

Without a genuine blank, the forger must use a copying machine to make a duplicate of the registration certificate and then white out the information on it before making another copy. There will be a space where the photograph was, but it's easy to cover this with a slightly larger photograph for the forgery. However, anyone looking at the back of the paper will see that the printing is missing under the photograph, which will be a clue to the forgery.

It's also possible to mutilate the original and remove the photograph by cutting the tape along the edges of the picture with a razor knife. This allows reproducing the entire form. The copy is then filled out as described above.

A slightly harder photo-I.D. to fake is the New York City Firearms Control Board permit card. This is printed in light green ink on card stock, with a security pattern to show erasures and alterations. This ink does rub off with an eraser.

On the right is the owner's photograph, held on with a strip of tape two inches wide, enough to seal the edges completely. Under the tape and overlapping out to the right edge of the card is an embossed seal. The tape and photograph are not themselves embossed. Information is typed into the spaces provided.

The back of the card is printed with rules covering the issuance of the permit, a space for the owner's signature, and spaces for the new address. There is no pattern printed on the back.

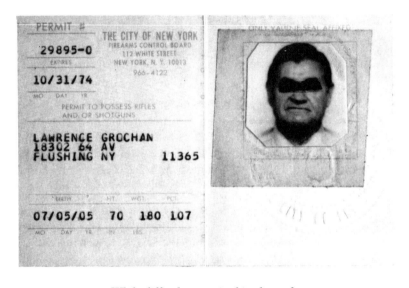

While difficult to see in this photo, the Firearms Control Board permit card has a light green pattern that shows erasures and alterations.

Forging this card requires one of two starts. The easy way is for the forger to obtain a blank from the agency, and take it home. The second way is for the forger to typeset and print the card from scratch, which is not as difficult as it seems. The green ink makes it very difficult to make a litho negative without using a filter and pan-chromatic film, which makes typesetting the simplest course. In any case, the security pattern would make it hard to remove the typed data.

The herringbone security pattern is, surprisingly, commonly available in transfer type. Photographing it with litho film and superimposing the pattern onto the type is simple, requiring only a double exposure to make a duplicate negative. This negative then serves to make the printing plate.

Making a litho negative of the back side is possible, and easier than photographing the face of the card. However, it's typical for forgers to have the back side typeset too, so that the type on the front and back matches.

Altering later-generation photo-I.D. is not as easy, because governments learned from their early mistakes and made the I.D. one piece. There are several ways forgers get around this problem, though.

The first is "quick and dirty." Let's say a kid needs to add a couple of years to the age on his drivers license to get into bars. This type of forgery won't pass for anything except a hurried inspection under bad light, but this is typical for bars.

He obtains a duplicate drivers license, claiming that he lost the original. He uses the original for surgery, and keeps the duplicate for use while driving, because a police officer will be very likely to spot any alterations.

If it's a laminated license, he splits the plastic with a razor blade. Once he has the plastic split, he can add or change numbers with a fine brush and a bottle of Spotone photographic dye. If the card is a photograph of a hand-written application, he shouldn't have much trouble matching his own hand-writing. If it's typed, he'll have to be vary careful. Once the license reads the way he wants it, he re-seals it with a hot iron or super glue.

Replacing the photograph in a drivers license is more difficult. The replacement photograph is actually in an "emulsion," which is the top layer of a piece of photographic paper. This layer must be separated from the paper backing using a very sharp, single-edged razor blade. Likewise, only the top layer of the piece of photo-I.D. being altered must be removed. It is replaced with the new photograph, and the laminate is then sealed. This procedure does not result in the raised panel that occurs if one photo is pasted on top of another — which is a dead give-away.

One way forgers disguise alterations in laminated cards is by scuffing the plastic. Dropping it on pavement and rubbing it back and forth with the foot is one way it's done.

A quick way to make a fake I.D. is to borrow a friend's license, paste new information lightly over the card, then take a photo for a new card. When the forger's done, he carefully pulls the information he added and returns the card to his friend.

There is another type of quick and dirty license forgery that has been seen in some circumstances. Let's say our forger borrows a friend's drivers license for a couple of hours, promising to return it undamaged.

He needs a color photograph of himself to fit in the space on the drivers license. He'll also need lettering spelling out the details he wishes to change. He might be trying to create a new identity, or he might be making a copy of his own drivers license with a different date of birth. If he's merely altering the date on his own license, it's much easier.

He cuts out and pastes-up the items he needs to alter onto the borrowed license. He uses wax, not water paste, for adhesive so he won't damage the license. If he doesn't have the right sort of wax, he might use a light coating of rubber cement. He covers the paste-up with a sheet of clean glass to ensure that everything lies flat.

He'll also need a Polaroid camera with a close-up lens that gives one-to-one reproduction. In other words, the photo he takes of the altered license must be the same size as the original.

The paste-up is laid on a flat surface, and the camera and tripod are set up over it. He'll probably have to use a flash bounced off a nearby sheet of white paper for illumination. A direct flash won't work in most cases because it's too bright and will "burn out" the picture. Room light is not good enough, either, because incandescent and many fluorescent lights are the wrong "color temperature." This gives the wrong color balance to the print, and it will appear too brown or even greenish.

He makes an exposure and waits for the print to develop. If it's too dark, he increases the exposure by adjusting the camera or bringing the sheet of reflective paper closer. If the print is too light (burned out), he reduces the exposure if the camera has adjustments. If not, he places the sheet of white paper farther away or places one layer of a handkerchief over the lens of the flash unit.

When he gets a good print, he cuts it out to the same size as the original license. This is the quick and very "dirty" version. One flaw is that the backing of the print doesn't match the reverse side of the license. Many states issue licenses with printing on the back to defeat this sort of forgery. The chances are that the color and finish of the reverse side of the print won't even approach the quality of the real article.

One method used to duplicate the printing on the back of a photo I.D. card involves obtaining self-sticking labels from an office supply store large enough to cover the back of the license. A small rubber stamp kit can be used to make up a stamp that will reproduce the official printing. The stamp will then reproduce the necessary information on the label which covers the back of the Polaroid forgery.

This sort of crude forgery is only useful to a forger when flashed from inside a plastic I.D. holder. This might fool a store clerk when paying with a check. It might fool a librarian when applying for a library card. It won't ever fool a police officer because the first thing he'll ask the forger is to take it out of his wallet.

*A life-size drivers license will look the right
size in a Polaroid photo taken by a forger.*

An elaborate method of concocting a crude forgery is making a giant-size I.D. card background that can be taped to a wall while the forger photographs himself standing in front of it. If he's doing a drivers license, he doesn't have to borrow a real one. He can simply go to the local office of the motor vehicle bureau and pick up an application card. The clerks hand these out freely because they aren't valid as licenses. Using this as a model, the forger draws the boxes on a large sheet of white bristol board. He'll need type to simulate the printed lines. He can get this typeset, or use "press type" if it's available in a large enough size. Another way it's done is to set the lines in the proper type face from "press-type" and have them enlarged at a graphics shop.

Once the card replica is complete, the forger stands in front of it and photographs himself using a self-timer. He uses a flash, placed about a foot high and to one side, because that's how the flash is set up on most photo I.D. cameras. He then cuts the print out, and he's got a crude I.D.

One reason it's crude is that it lacks the validation stamps and seals. The *I.D. Checking Guide* lists the validations and shows a color illustration of every state's license. In some cases, the state seal or a security number overlaps the photograph.

Forgers get around this by using a rubber stamp to print the seal and signature, as well as any numbers that are required. Once the card is laminated, it is very hard to tell that the stamp and seal aren't in the photographic emulsion.

Why do forgers prefer Polaroid? Why not a standard 35mm camera and color negative film, with prints from the photo-finisher? This other method is recommended by Rex Feral in a book on the subject.[3] He suggests that because photofinishing today is done by automated machinery, the forger is safe from discovery. That's correct. The machinery can't call the cops. However, the prints are packaged by people. While many of the clerks working as photo-finishers are tired, overworked, underpaid, and uninterested in anything but quitting time, most forgers don't want to bet their freedom that one of them won't be a Dudley Do-Right.

There are many types of color negative film and color printing paper that can be processed at home with kits of the proper chemicals. There is no way to learn the entire technique from a book. If you're seriously interested in this subject, take a course in color photography at a junior college.

The advantage to the forger of using the color negative-positive process is that color printing paper looks more like the material used to make photo-I.D. than does Polaroid. The printing paper typically has a paper back, instead of a glossy black or white plastic back. The paper is also thinner, and feels more like genuine photo I.D. The paper's emulsion, the coating that holds the photograph, is more absorbent, unlike the faces of the instant prints. This makes placing stamps or inked notations over the photo much easier.

Limited Use

No matter how good a forgery may look, it will stand only limited exposure. Successful forgers must stay within the limits, and avoid over-confidence. With patience and luck, they slowly build up a new persona in order to obtain genuine I.D. to replace the ones they've faked.

Sources

1. *Check & Credit Card Fraud Prevention Manual,* Los Angeles, CA, 1984, p. 106.
2. *Centurion,* November, 1983. p. 43.
3. *How To Rip Off A Drug Dealer,* Rex Feral, Boulder, CO, Paladin Press, 1984, p. 139.

10

Professional Services

Forgers don't do everything by themselves. They're not likely to have all of the tools, and they're also not likely to have all of the skills. There are several types of professional services they might use in preparing some of their bogus documentation.

Printing

The simplest need is for business cards in the forger's name. Let's say our forger has picked up a card in his travels, that says:

BLOWHARD INSURANCE BROKERS
2314 East 23 Street
Midtown, Iowa, 12345
Joe Blowhard, Broker

He wants a batch of cards printed, but with his name instead of Joe's. This is the sort of job that a printer gets every day of the week. The eye of suspicion will not be upon him when he places his order. He simply tells the printer that he's the new salesman, and that he needs a thousand cards with his name on them instead of his boss's.

A complication might come if the printer gets the order finished before the promised day or time. This rarely happens, but if it does, he might call the number listed on the card to inform the forger that his cards are ready. When the forger shows up, the printer might tell him that when he made the call, the person who answered the telephone told him that nobody by that name worked there. The forger's response?

He just smiles and says: "Yeah, I know. She's new, too. Started the day after I did."

It's also possible to have a printer print up a batch of baptismal certificates. While baptismal certificate blanks are obtainable in religious supply stores, they look better and more impressive if they're printed with the name of the church at the top. Printers have stock books of certificate blanks, from which their customers can make a choice. If the printer asks why the church is out of town, the forger can tell him that he was born there, and that this will be a donation to the church when he goes back to visit.

Forgers can get almost anything they want printed commercially. Printers are in the trade for the money, and don't question customers when they give them work. The only restrictions affecting printers are those involving currency and government documents. It's illegal to print money, or to copy most government documents. The U.S. Secret Service distributes brochures to printers listing the papers that are illegal to copy. Birth certificates are not among them. The only other concern to printers is pornography, especially that involving children.

Photocopying

This is probably the most useful service to forgers because they can copy almost anything adequately and for a very low cost. The best sort of copy shops for this sort of activity are those with self-service machines. This allows the forger to run copies without anyone else seeing them. Although copy machine operators, like printers, aren't overly curious, there's some security in not having others involved in the copying.

Copy machines vary in the quality of the copies they turn out. Many are adequate, but some turn out only faded copies, hardly suitable for forgery. Those shops using machines by Canon and Xerox usually turn out the best reproductions.

Typesetting

When the forger needs a document made up from scratch, he usually tries to get the printing typeset. A skilled calligrapher might try doing it with a brush and ink. But most try to have it professionally typeset.

The main reason has to do with quality. Unless he's trying to forge a birth certificate from the turn of the century, the quality of the type has to look good. A typewriter can't do it. A "desktop publishing" program on a computer can't do it as well as a photo-typesetting machine.

The hardest challenge comes when the forger needs a line of type to match a document that he's altering. While a gifted artist may be able to match type by hand and draw each letter with a fine brush, most forgers don't have this level of skill. Modern photo-typesetting, on the other hand, can match any typestyle or size.

Graphic Services

Forgeries often require that artwork be reproduced. A logo on an invoice might need to be reduced to fit a business card. Several copies of an original document may be required, so they can be cut and pasted to fit different needs. This is the sort of work provided by a graphics services shop.

The graphics shop uses a large camera, known as a "process" camera, to photograph documents and artwork. The process camera can reproduce the material at same size, or it can enlarge or reduce it by a factor of between two and four.

Another service obtainable is paste-up. Unless the forger is working on official government documents, he probably won't have any problem getting a professional paste-up artist to assemble his art-work. The few dollars it costs will be less than the cost of the equipment he'd need to do it himself.

Engraving

Engraving is a dying art, but it's still useful for making name-plates and embossing dies. This process is called "photo-engraving," as distinct from hand engraving. In photo-engraving, the technician makes a high-contrast litho negative of the artwork, which can be a seal, signature, or any combination of art and type. He exposes an engraving plate using the negative, and etches the plate with an acid mixture. The result is a positive on the plate, and this can be used for stamping or embossing.

To fit an embossing machine, it's necessary to cut the die to size. This can be specified when the printing is ordered.

Walking Through a Job

Let's walk through a job to see how these services are used by forgers to create phony credentials. Let's say that our forger has a business card from the "Eagle Meat Packing Company" in Iowa City.

He needs a letter of recommendation from this company to support listing them as previous employers. A letter on their stationery might forestall a telephone call that might disclose that he never worked there. To create the letterhead, he first needs to get the eagle logo enlarged, or "blown up."

The business card is about 3½" wide, and standard letterhead paper is 8½" wide. The eagle measures 3" wide from wing-tip to wing-tip. For the letterhead, the eagle should be about 7" wide, or enlarged by 233%. This is what the graphic shop can do. He asks for a "PMT," or a "VELOX," of the eagle at 233%. Technically, a VELOX and a PMT are different but, for these purposes, either will do. The PMT will probably cost less.

He will probably want to keep the type the same size, but arrange it differently on the letterhead. For this, he'll also need a PMT of the business card at 100%.

EAGLE MEAT PACKING COMPANY
1234 Smedley Street   Iowa City IA, 12345

Telephone   Richard Unreal
123-4567   Manager

Any business card a forger picks up
could be his own if he knows a little about printing.

Finally, he'll need a paste-up of the new letterhead to give to the printer. He can do this himself, if he's adept with an X-Acto knife and a grid sheet, or he can have it done professionally for a few dollars.

Another service available from a graphics shop is screening prints. If our forger has a photograph that he'd like to insert into a newspaper article photocopy, he needs it "screened." This means that a technician re-photographs it with a process camera and a half-tone screen to produce a print made up of dots of various sizes, to simulate the different shades of gray. This is how photographs are printed in newspapers, magazines, and books.

Half-tone screens are classified by the number of lines of dots per inch they produce. One that has 85 lines of dots per inch is called, an "85-line screen." Many newspapers use this screen, but some use a coarser one, a 65-line screen. To get a half-tone print to match a newspaper article, a technician must see it to match the screen.

To get his name inserted into the article, the forger will require photo-typesetting. Most newspapers use only a few type styles. The most common are *Crown* and *Century*. Somewhat less often used is *Times*. These are standard type fonts that typesetters normally keep in stock.

*The paste-up lines on this
letterhead won't show when it gets printed.*

11

Quality Control

Most forgers are not very masterful. They make obvious mistakes or omissions that can be easily spotted by trained eyes. The following is a checklist of obvious errors found in many forgeries:

- All of the documents are nice and crisp. They look as if they all were acquired the same day. When some are aged, it looks more natural.

- The same photo is used on two or more pieces of I.D. This is a sure tip-off to anyone who sees them.

- The physical description on the I.D. doesn't match the person presenting it.

- I.D. cards are evenly dirty, or dirtier at the edges. If they were aged by rubbing dirt into them, chances are it was rubbed in uniformly. This, too, is a give-away.

- Obvious erasures are a tell-tale sign. So, too, are areas that vary in lightness or darkness, or raised edges.

- Look at the signature block on the back of a plastic credit card. Is the block raised so that you can easily feel it with a fingertip? This happens when forgers glue another one on and can be detected when the card is taken out of its plastic holder.

*Using an identical photograph on two
different pieces of I.D. is a sure tip-off to fraud.*

- What about the pattern? MasterCards have a pattern printed on the signature block. Does it show erasures?

- View the card by reflected light. Can you see any indented lines or irregularities that shouldn't be there? If so, it's probably a forgery.

*Sloppy handiwork can easily be detected, as with
this photo crudely pasted over the original picture.*

- Is the lettering and numbering in the right place? It's easy for forgers to slip, especially with an embossing machine, and place a line of type too high or too low.

- Are there any errors in spelling? This seems stupid, but some forgers get caught this way.

- Is the wrong signature used to validate the document? Did they use the governor's signature when the commissioner's is required?

- Does the photo look enough like the person presenting it? They may be using someone else's I.D.

- If you ask the person to sign their name, do they hesitate? Hesitation, as if the person is uncertain or nervous about writing their own name, should tip off an alert clerk.

- Many forgers don't bother to memorize all of the information on the I.D. they're trying to pass. A simple trick some cops like to use is to take the I.D. and ask the person his or her birthdate or address. Is there other I.D. in their wallet to support the main piece?

*The numbers on this credit card are too low —
a clear indication that the card is a forgery.*

12

How Forgers
Pass Fake I.D.

Manufacturing fake I.D. is only the forger's first step. "Passing" it is the next step. In some cases, it's "Mission Impossible." In others, it's surprisingly easy.

Let's lay out the forger's first rule of passing fake I.D.:

It can't be used in situations in which it's easy to check it out. A forgery may be technically perfect, but will never pass in some circumstances. One is the faked drivers license when stopped by the police. Twenty years ago, it would have been possible to fake a license and have it accepted, but the combination of the radio and the computer has made this almost impossible today. Police officers routinely do a radio check of the drivers license and vehicle registration by radio with the department of motor vehicles. This has two parts. One is to confirm that such paperwork has actually been issued. This can only happen if the license is real and the department has a record of it. The second part is a check for "wants." This is to discover if the license has been reported lost, the vehicle stolen, or if the person has outstanding arrest warrants against him.

Limits & Dangers

From this, you can understand the limits of false I.D. Even selecting a very common name, such as "John Smith" isn't much help to the forger because of the other identifiers listed on the license and stored in the central computer's memory. He'd have to match the birth-date of a real "John Smith" and have the same address. This brings us to another pitfall.

Buying fake I.D. or stolen I.D. is extremely risky. This is true even if the I.D. is genuine and with a photo that closely resembles the purchaser. One risk is that the seller will denounce the purchaser to the police. Police organizations the world over have their informers, some of which are petty criminals whom they permit to operate because they lead them to major offenders. The street-wise forger will happily sell stolen or faked I.D., then pass the buyer's name to the cops.[1]

Another pitfall is that of stolen I.D. The theft may have been reported to the police. This puts the thief out in the open if he tries to use it.

Another pitfall is being given I.D. from someone who is wanted for a serious crime. Criminals on the run often procure false papers from a street dealer. Sometimes, turning in the genuine I.D. is part of the deal. The fugitive has no further need for the genuine papers. The dealer gives the wanted person a "discount" because he knows that he can re-sell the papers to an unsuspecting client. The unsuspecting client can find himself under arrest for a serious crime the first time he tries to show his new drivers license to a police officer.

Presenting False I.D.

Fake I.D. cards are often carried in a wallet. Certificates and diplomas are usually kept in an envelope because that is the normal way to carry them.

A wallet with a plastic card folder is ideal for the forger. They are both inexpensive and commonly available. The plastic envelope helps cover up scratches and other irregularities which might disclose the forgery. This is one reason why police officers ask people to take their cards out of their wallets.

Practical Uses

The exact use to which fake I.D. is put is probably the most important factor in the forger's success. Using a genuine, but altered, drivers license to get into a bar is a very common use. This works only if there's no distinctive mark on the license which identifies a minor, such as being photographed in profile. This is standard in both Maryland and Nevada, for example. Another distinction is a different color background for minors, such as the red color used in Delaware.

Passing out-of-state papers is the safest use. It's easy for a forger to pretend that he's just arrived from another state. Bar bouncers are usually dull, brutish, and insensitive, and certainly don't know the distinctions and quirks of I.D. documents from all 50 states and Canada. In a bar's dim light, a bouncer is not likely to notice whether a photo has a red or brown background.

Those forging out-of-state I.D., especially drivers licenses, choose the state carefully. Michigan, for example, uses retroreflective lamination and this is not the easiest to fake. Florida uses a state seal visible only under ultra-violet light. It's unlikely that a gatekeeper at a bar will be equipped with either a UV lamp or a retroreflective viewer, but there are often other security measures used on these cards. For example, Florida licenses also use a state seal and a code number overlapping the driver's photograph.

Bank and credit cards provide excellent backup I.D. for the forger. Even one that's totally faked, and lacking the magnetic stripe, will work for I.D. when cashing a check. The forger's technique is simple:

He writes a check in front of the clerk, who usually will ask for two forms of I.D. If one has a photograph, the other can be almost anything. The forger flips open his wallet to the plastic card section. The clerk will simply copy the number, without ever taking the cards out for close examination. The reason is that this is all the clerk is ever required to do to cover him- or herself.[2]

The implication of this procedure is amazing. It means that the forger only has to forge one side of the bank card. The rear, with its hard-to-copy magnetic stripe and patterned signature block, is never viewed by the clerk if the card is kept back-to-back with the drivers license. Likewise, the forged drivers license, possibly lacking a retroreflective lamination and a state seal, doesn't get a close examination. The clerk never checks for any printing on the back.

Using fake I.D. to rent post office boxes is also common. Postal clerks never scrutinize licenses and bank cards closely. Like all low-level bureaucrats, they're only interested in covering their backsides and protecting their jobs by writing down the numbers they're required to record.

Private postal box operators, who rent mail drops, are likewise uninterested in crusading for genuine I.D. Mail drops are profitable enterprises, and any operator who is too rigorous in demanding I.D. is simply turning away business. Most mail drop operators display a healthy lack of curiosity about clients.

Opening bank accounts and renting safe deposit boxes are easy tasks. In some cases, customers don't even have to show I.D., but merely write their address and Social Security number on an application.

Using fake papers to procure genuine ones is easy, as long as the fakes don't show evidence of forgery. That's why many forgers use photocopies of documents rather than original forgeries. It's impossible to prove that a photocopy is of an altered or false document without having a real one for comparison or checking with the originating office. Birth certificates from other states are almost always accepted. Even clerks at a government office don't know all of the different forms of documents issued in the country.

Attitude is as critical to the forger's success as paperwork. If he doesn't feel confident, it's hard to fake it. Nervousness might be a tip-off to a state bureau clerk, if it's noticed.

If the forger is challenged, he usually has nothing to fear. The worst that's likely to happen is that the clerk will tell him that the I.D. is not acceptable. If this happens, he might say something like, "It's perfectly all right in my home state." If he's asked for another piece of I.D. to support it, he can show something else, even if it's a library card. If he doesn't have a drivers license, he can explain this by saying he's from New York City, or Chicago, where public transport is so commonly available that many people don't drive.

Many forgers overcome nervousness by going through several dry runs first, to quench the apprehension. If the forger's objective is a genuine drivers license based upon a fake birth certificate, he might try to obtain a library card first. Practically nobody tries to obtain library cards under false pretenses, which is why he's far less likely to run into trouble.

Another easy path used for obtaining supporting I.D. is registering at a junior college. Because most of them charge tuition, all that's required is money. The only situation in which the forger's identity and residence would get close scrutiny is if the instruction is tuition-free for residents. Otherwise, hand over your money, fill out the forms, and the school will usually issue a photo-I.D. Usually, these have a serial number, enhancing their authenticity.

Getting a non-critical I.D. serves the forger two ways. It helps build up his confidence, and the newly-acquired genuine I.D. can be used to support impersonation, replacing a forged document with a genuine one.

Sources

1. *How To Disappear Completely and Never Be Found,* Doug Richmond, Port Townsend, WA, Loompanics Unlimited, 1986, pp. 67-68.

2. Personal experience of the author. In writing thousands of checks in several states over several decades, it's never been necessary to take the I.D. out of the wallet for close scrutiny.

13

Banking and Other Financial Concerns

To support a false identity, a forger may need to purchase materials and supplies from out of town. Sending a money order may seem suspicious for some purchases. On the other hand, a business check gives the aura of authenticity.

Establishing a business checking account isn't very difficult. Some think that a bank will necessarily need some sort of official paperwork such as a business license.[1] This isn't necessarily so. There are certain businesses for which a license is not required. Freelance journalism or consulting are two examples. By adopting a business name, such as "Smedley's Professional Services," the forger can have his checks imprinted with it.

Banks require a social security number to open an account, but not a card. The forger can simply memorize a bogus number and recite it if asked, without having to forge the card. The odds are overwhelming that nobody will ever ask for the social security number verbally. There will be a space for it on several of the forms that must be filled out, and all the forger has to do is write it in.

An important matter is the address provided. A box number gives the impression of having something to hide. Reputable businesses with post office boxes usually list their box numbers first, and their street address on the line below. This way, the postal service directs the mail to the box, but the customer or supplier has a geographical address for UPS shipments or visits.

Today's bankers don't act like the stereotypical bankers of old. They're doing their best to be modern merchandisers, and try to sell as many of their banking services as they can. This modern attitude helps forgers gather additional I.D.[2] With a bank account, they can get a check cashing card, as well as other magic plastic that rounds out the image they're trying to cultivate.

The forger can take advantage of this greed by responding to as many of the mail-order credit card offers as he can. This "shotgun" strategy pays off because there is no universally-followed system of checking references by banks and credit card companies. It's still possible to obtain a genuine piece of plastic by mail without providing any genuine references because some companies are so greedy for the business that they don't bother to check out applicants. In other cases, there are quotas and "contests" for bank employees, to build up sales, and employees will often cut corners to build up their personal account lists.

Sources

1. *New I.D. in America,* Anonymous, Boulder, CO, Paladin Press, 1983, p. 74.

2. *Ibid.,* pp. 31-35.

14

Impersonation

For a specific reason, or just for fun, a forger might want to set up his fake I.D. so that he can impersonate a doctor or lawyer. This might seem to be an extremely dangerous step, but actually it's not.

There are strict laws in every state regarding practicing medicine or law without a license. The key is "practicing." You can say that you're a doctor, but as long as you don't treat anybody, or try to perform surgery, you're perfectly legal.

Strangely, it's easier to impersonate a doctor than it is to impersonate most other types. There's a certain aura of respect surrounding doctors, and this intimidates many people. When a doctor orders stationery from a printer, you can be sure that the printer won't ask to see his medical license.

Forgers can order subscriptions to every medical magazine they wish, to help bolster the image. Carrying a couple of these around helps establish the fake identity. It's also fairly easy to open a bank account, although in keeping with the "profession," the impersonator should kick it off with quite a few thousand dollars.

Joining the county or state medical society is also possible. The impersonator simply explains that he's not licensed in the state, because he's doing private research instead of holding a practice. The most that can happen is that they'll refuse to accept him. It's not illegal to try to join the county medical society.

The critical point for the impersonator is to avoid ever treating anyone for anything, no matter how small. He might find himself in a bind if someone becomes critically ill or has an accident, and people who know him as a doctor call upon him to administer emergency care. He might be able to slip out of this by explaining that he's "not that sort" of a doctor. Another explanation, which people today will understand readily, is that he's not in practice and doesn't carry malpractice insurance, and that he won't touch anyone for fear of being sued.

Similarly, impersonators can claim to be accountants, attorneys, or other professional persons. They simply avoid practicing the alleged "profession" to avoid troubles with the law.

15

Employment

There are two sides to the question of employment. The first is how the forger benefits from a job he already has. There are some jobs that help people get the inside track on acquiring new I.D.

Inside Jobs

Working for a government agency gets the forger on the inside track. No, it doesn't have to be the C.I.A. or the F.B.I. How many people need I.D. that lets them pass for an F.B.I. or C.I.A. agent, anyway?

The sort of government job that helps the forger is the one in which he has access to documents and document blanks. If he always takes home a few blanks, even if they're just letterheads and printed envelopes, he will soon have a forgery stash. If he works for any government record-keeping agency, he'll have access to blanks. Because of the elaborate cross-referencing system any government agency keeps, he'll also have access to forms from other government agencies. For example, someone working for the U.S. passport office will get to see birth certificates from every state in the Union, and most foreign countries. This gives him a chance to make photocopies for his own use.

Those working for the U. S. Government Printing Office have a free ride to everything in the shop. The printing of currency is closely guarded, but many other government printing jobs are done without tight security.

State, county, and local governments all have documents that can be useful to the forger. A job in the motor vehicle bureau, or department of transportation, provides access to drivers licenses and vehicle registrations.

The state or county birth and death registry is a happy hunting ground for anyone intent on acquiring fake I.D. Not only will they have access to forms, but they'll also have access to records, which allows them to match up with someone their age for extra backstopping. An employee there could also sell information without risk to those who need a match-up with an actual person for "papertripping."

Governments aren't the only sources of information or material for forgeries. A happy hunting ground is a job in a company that produces plastic card blanks for a bank or retailer. While trying to make off with dozens or hundreds may be impossible, pocketing one or two is simple.

Working in a hospital provides the opportunity to get inside information and documentation, too. Employees get to see birth and death certificates. In addition, patients often leave valuables, including documents, with hospital staff for safekeeping.

Even a clerical job with a stationer, office supply firm, or paper company gives access to document blanks that few ever get. The exact nature of the blanks will depend upon the company, but if there's anything that's not in stock, employees can get it through a special order with the suppliers.

Any sort of clerical job with a retailer allows one to get genuine bank card numbers and expiration dates. Because this is a wide-open avenue for thieves, many retailers have adopted the policy of requiring their employees to ask the customer if he or she wants the carbons of the charge card form. This is to forestall theft by rummaging through the firm's garbage. Not all customers want them, and one or two carbons can provide enough raw material for several forgeries.

A job in a print shop teaches the hands-on skills that are needed to generate documents from scratch. If a printer has a contract to supply any sort of document blanks or printed forms to a government agency, an employee could skim off a few for his own purposes.

Silk-screening is a process for producing signs and other graphics that is also applicable for forgeries. Learning the basic skill, and using the shop's equipment, gives a forger a start in producing bank cards and other plastic I.D.

Likewise for employment as a typesetter. Typesetting has changed from the old days of Linotype machines and hand-set type. Today's equipment uses photo-typesetting, and is far more versatile. Modern typesetting machines are computers that include graphics programs. This means they can reproduce, on photographic paper, any conceivable form or design. The latest models of Varityper, Itek, and Compugraphic have disc memories to store material after it has been composed. This means it can be saved and used to turn out additional copies at a later date.

Another advantage for the forger of working in a print shop is that he has access to equipment that he probably could never afford to buy. He can make use of this equipment during off-hours. If he has a key, he may be able to enter the shop on weekends for a little unofficial work. Typically, other employees won't be very curious about what he's doing.[1]

A special point about doing personal work is the employer's attitude. Some don't care. Those who do are only concerned about large volume. They know that some employees may do secret jobs at night, printing a thousand letterheads for a client of their own. This is why they'll look for the big shortages. A box of envelopes, or a thousand sheets of paper, makes a dent that they might notice. Nobody will be aware of five sheets skimmed off to run fake birth certificates.

Exploiting Opportunities

Finally, almost any sort of employment can provide the forger with the opportunity to build toward his goals. He'll come into contact with letters, purchase orders, invoices, and other business documents. All of these, especially from other companies, are raw material for forgeries. A letter from a company which would look good on an employment application can provide the letterhead for a letter of recommendation. It also provides the name of someone who works there, and a sample of the signature.

Using Fake I.D. To Get a Job

There are many ways forgers can use fake I.D. to help get a job, and several methods of testing its effectiveness. Once the forger has assembled his fake I.D. and cover story, he might try them out on a job he really doesn't want, so that if there are any serious errors, they won't cost him. He can use the feedback from the interview to help him detect weak points in his story or documentation.

What Employers Seek

Generally, they're looking for people who are capable and reliable, and willing to work for what they pay. For this, they'll ask for an employment history and may require an application listing education and past employment.

For some jobs, resumes, applications, and other paperwork are not required. Many agricultural and construction jobs are like this. People show up, are hired on the spot, and if they don't work out, they're canned. Period. No problems, no complications.

Those people foreign-born, who have an accent, may have to show a card or other I.D. to be hired. Federal authorities are cracking down on employers who hire illegal labor. This is where a fake card can help gain employment for a forger.

Employment Applications

Forgers fired from a previous job, or who spent time in jail, may find it difficult to cover all the gaps in their employment. In some fields, a reasonable explanation is to claim that the time was spent "consulting."[2] This may be true for accountants, engineers, and college professors, but it's hard to explain how a butcher or auto mechanic can spend time consulting.

Gaps can also be covered by claiming fake employment. This ruse can be supported by attaching copies of falsified letters of recommendation. To get a particular job, other types of forgeries may be used. One is the fake newspaper article.

This ruse requires an article from an out-of-town newspaper. The article might be a "puff piece" on an individual who is about the forger's age. This person may have been awarded a "Man of the Year" trophy, or some other honor. The forger substitutes his own photo and name, as described in the section on forgery techniques, and claims the honor himself.

In some cases, it is necessary to combine a piece of paper and a "cover story" to provide the right effect. Let's say our forger has been in prison for 18 months. He wants to cover this gap, and doesn't feel secure enough to do it by adjusting the dates of his real employment because someone might check. Consequently, he's got to fill the 18-month gap with something totally false.

For this, he might choose a company halfway across the continent. He makes up a phony letter of recommendation and photocopies it, then attaches the copy to his application. To deter any phone calls which might check this "employment," he must make it for something totally out of his line. If he's applying for a job as a butcher, he might make this imaginary job that of a roofer. When the interviewer asks why he went to Iowa City to become a roofer, he says:

"My mother was there dying of cancer. I had to go to take care of her. I had no job, and not much in savings. My mother's neighbor felt sorry for me, so he gave me a job as a roofer in his company, to help pay the bills. I wasn't very good at it, but he kept me on because he felt sorry for me. When my mother finally died, I left."

This combination is likely to work because there's little point in making a long-distance call to verify employment that's not relevant to the present job. If, however, he was applying for a job which requires a security clearance, this story would never work.

Sources

1. Personal experience of the author's when he worked in a printing shop. Other employees were too busy running jobs of their own, or getting drunk or stoned, to care.

2. *The Disappearing Book, Vol. 2,* Kailua, Hawaii, Morrison Peterson Publishing Inc., pp. 10-12.

16

Further Reading

I.D. CHECKING GUIDE

Published each year by the Drivers License Guide Company, 1492 Oddstad Drive, Redwood City, CA 94063. Toll-free number: (800) 227-8827.

This is a fully-illustrated four-color guide to drivers licenses for the United States and Canada. A supplement shows licenses issued in overseas American territories such as Samoa and Guam. A short section covers bank cards and another discusses auto license plates and their validation stickers.

This is an excellent guide for the forger because it lists explicitly many of the security checks used on licenses, as well as number coding systems, where used. The color illustrations are top-quality reproductions of the official documents.

Single copies are about $20.00 each.

U.S. IDENTIFICATION MANUAL

Published each year by the Drivers License Guide Company, 1492 Oddstad Drive, Redwood City, CA 94063. Toll-free number: (800) 227-8827.

This is a large, 8½″ x 11″ loose-leaf guide to official identity documents, designed for periodic supplements to keep it up to date. This publication has sections for drivers licenses, auto registrations, official government agency documents, immigration cards, and bank and credit cards.

This book contains much more than the forger needs to know, and is valuable mainly because it contains everything he might possibly want to know. Various sections contain the names and addresses of state agencies, including departments of transportation and law enforcement agencies.

Single copies cost about $100.00 each.

ACCESS CONTROL SYSTEMS

This book, by Michael C. DiMeo, General Manager of Cardkey, is published by Cardkey Systems, 20660 Bahama Street, Chatsworth, CA 91311. Telephone: (213) 998-2777.

This is a non-technical guide to access control systems that provides the forger with a good description of the security measures used by manufacturers of card entry systems and card locks. The main value of this book is as warning of some of the sophisticated devices used as security enhancers by the suppliers of access control systems. One obvious point learned from this book is that it's remarkably easy to forge a company I.D. badge but very difficult to use it to open an electronic lock. Such a forgery is useful as auxiliary identification, though.

THE PAPER TRIP, I and II

Published by Eden Press, Inc., P.O. Box 8410, Fountain Valley, CA 92708.

These two books, by Barry Reid, are valuable both for the practical information and for the historical overview they provide. *PAPER TRIP I* is the book which started it all, and which led to congressional hearings on the ease with which one can acquire genuine government I.D. under false pretenses. These hearings led to a largely ineffective law, and resulted in the publication of *PAPER TRIP II,* which lays out methods used to defeat that law.

PAPER TRIP II also contains a short practical guide to forgery, with reproductions of various I.D. components.

CHECK AND CREDIT CARD FRAUD
PREVENTION MANUAL

Published by Bob Cekosky, 3219 Descanso Drive, P.O. Box 261118, Los Angeles, CA 90026-0118. Telephone: (213) 666-1099.

The main value of this book is the detailed listing of investigative techniques used by company credit and security officers when they check out I.D. and credit applications. A careful study of these pages will provide the reader a gold mine of do's and dont's.

This book contains a wealth of practical and technical information. Pages 190 and 191 have a detailed explanation of the "retroreflective" lamination system that embosses an invisible seal into the plastic used in laminating photo-I.D. cards, and the instrument used to view the seal.

YOU WILL ALSO WANT TO READ: